Prostitution in Elizabethan and Jacobean Comedy

Prostitution in Elizabethan and Jacobean Comedy

by

Anne M. Haselkorn

The Whitston Publishing Company
Troy, New York
1983

FOR

Howard and Danny

ACKNOWLEDGMENTS

I am extremely grateful for the generous help of Dr. Leonora L. Brodwin, the mentor for my Ph.D. dissertation, the seminal work for this book. I am also deeply indebted to both Dr. Betty Travitsky and Dorothy Litt for their sound advice, unfailing support, and limitless patience.

I would like to acknowledge the kind assistance of the staffs of St. John's Library, the Queens College Library, and the New York Public Library.

Anne M. Haselkorn

CONTENTS

When the first letter of the terms Cavalier, Liberal and Puritan appears in upper case, it refers to the definition which I have appropriated for this study (see pp. 20-23). Other references to these terms are of a general nature, and the first letter appears in lower case.

INTRODUCTION

Prostitution, the oldest, if not the most honored profession, had, up until the seventeenth century, enjoyed a range of attitudes poised somewhere between severity and liberality. For centuries the institution was tolerated as a necessity but the prostitute was viewed as a moral pariah; the desire for her body was coupled with an abhorrence of the woman as whore. In spite of its increased liberality, the Renaissance continued to proclaim female chastity as an absolute—the fall of a woman heralded the corruption of her nature and automatically made a whore of her.

The word "whore" is practically synonymous with "prostitute." In the plays examined, a variety of other names appear— harlot, strumpet, punk (or pung), trull, wench, mutton, *bona roba*, quean, doxy, aunt, cockatrice, tweak, trug, mermaid, road, polecat, waistcoater, frump, stall, Dutch widow, Welsh virgin, etc.—but "whore" is the one most commonly used.

The limits of the term "whore" extend, in Renaissance drama, from the description of such a common professional as Alice in Jonson's *Bartholomew Fair* to the use of the word by Frank Thorney in *The Witch of Edmonton,* to describe his wife because she had married him, unaware that he already had a wife.[1] For the purposes of this study, "whore" and "prostitute" include the commercial practitioner who has sexual intercourse with a man who is not her husband, primarily for payment in money, land, clothes or jewels.

George R. Scott notes that the concubine is an unmarried woman who is a man's sexual partner, shares his house, and is maintained by him. Long before the English Renaissance, however, she was replaced in Europe by the mistress, who was maintained in a separate domicile, or the courtesan, who serviced the aristocrats. In charge of her own household, the courtesan was most discriminating in the selection of her lovers.[2]

In this study, two main types of women will be discussed: the courtesan and the common prostitute as they appear in Elizabethan and Jacobean comedy. Those who fall in the first category often arrive at their fallen state because they have been tempted into sin by seduction, or by a pimp, and then dropped, as Jane in *A Trick to Catch the Old One* (Middleton), the Country Wench in *Michaelmas Term* (Middleton), and Bellafront in *The Honest Whore, Parts I and II* (Dekker). In order to make their own way, these women are forced into a life of prostitution. These are the more ambitious prostitutes who have loftier ideas of becoming mistresses or wives. These whores form the bulwark of the main characters under discussion. The other type is comprised of hapless females, poverty-stricken and homeless, who have become harlots and must struggle to maintain themselves. Unlike the more enterprising prostitutes, these women do not look to the future but continue to service all clients until they have worn themselves out, and their persons are no longer marketable. These appear as background in *Measure for Measure* (Shakespeare), and in Bridewell in *The Honest Whore, Part II.* They are clearly common prostitutes—a socially irredeemable problem.

It is interesting that the treatment of the prostitute is a subject mainly dealt with in the comedies of the period. This might seem to suggest a lack of seriousness concerning the problem. However, while the intent of comedy is to delight, it also has a serious purpose, to instruct by exposing folly. Thus, the treatment of the prostitute in the comic mode permits such dramatists as Jonson, Shakespeare, Marston, Middleton and Dekker to examine serious concerns while eliciting laughter. And while tragedy deals with heroes and heroines on a grand scale, comedy concerns itself with ordinary people and their daily dilemmas.

To assess properly the role of the unchaste, fallen woman in the Renaissance and to discover her origins, it would be advisable to survey briefly the historic role of the prostitute and to demonstrate the conditions which influence the Renaissance view of the whore.

One aspect of the whore's history remains a constant: throughout medieval and modern times, she has been looked upon with contempt. Depending upon the moment in time, her situation has been attributed variously to evil, lustfulness, greed, economic hardship, or an unfavorable social environment.

In pagan times, a kind of formal intercourse was practiced as a rite to symbolize and ensure the fertility of crops and cattle.[3] This act in time became the special province of specific women whose duty it was to act as sacred prostitutes to the temples. They turned over to the temple the money that they received; however, after a time they were permitted to keep some for themselves. By the time of the Greeks, however, their position had reached bottom in the hierarchy of whores. Above them were the *auletrides*—flutists and dancers. The highest position was accorded the *hetairae,* courtesans of great beauty, charm and culture. The *hetairae* dispensed the largest share of pleasure and feminine companionship to the Greek male citizen, whose purpose for marriage was solely to create legitimate children. To name just a few famous Greek courtesans: the learned Aspasia later became the wife of Pericles; Bacchis was the mistress of Hyperides; Thargelia was the lover and confidant of Xerxes; Archaeanassa was the mistress of Plato. Generally, however, most Greek prostitutes had more limited opportunities and would not meet with such success. If they were slaves, many would become inmates of brothels known as *dicteria,* and they would be called *dicteriades,* receiving nothing for their services beyond food and clothing, the fees paid to them going to the State. The credit for the introduction of the first brothels in the West, in about 600 B.C., must go to the Athenian lawgiver, Solon. He instituted this public health service for all male citizens, justifying his action on the basis that prostitution was an "essential evil." This benevolence also resulted in a vast fortune for Solon.[4]

In the early Roman days, when virtue was the watchword of the Roman matron, the courtesan had an unencumbered field for the practice of her profession. At this time, the Romans must have regarded her with an esteem similar to that of the Greeks. The extant comedies of Plautus and Terence, based on Greek models, treat the whore sympathetically, and from these plays we may assume that this reflects a good deal of the attitude of the audience. Since courtesans could not enjoy the benefits of citizenship, one of which was the privilege of marrying a citizen, in many comic plots the dramatist revealed that the courtesan character actually had true civic status and thus could marry her lover. While the lack of citizenship for the courtesan was the prime barrier to the Roman marriage, in English Renaissance drama, the loss of a maidenhead would most effectively prevent her marriage. When the Renaissance writer wishes to set up opposition in a true love relationship, he often represents the "good girl" as apparently unchaste. When it is discovered that she is virtuous, the resolution is a happy one. In the following plays, the virgin is mistaken for a whore: Moll Cutpurse in *The Roaring Girl* (Middleton); The Governor of Bologna's sister Constantia in *The Chances* (Fletcher); and Marina in *Pericles* (Shakespeare).

The influx of amateur competition, however, created problems for the courtesan and resulted in a decided change in attitude toward her. The increase in adulterous relationships among the ruling classes during the disreputable period of the Empire are noted by Tacitus, a contemporary of Emperor Domitan (reigned A.D. 81-96). This ruler strongly favored female virtue and was highly critical of members of the upper class. To discourage wanton behavior, and according to custom, unchaste women had to publicly list themselves as prostitutes with the aediles. Avowal of such infamy, especially for upper-class women, was generally considered sufficient punishment. However, during Domitan's reign, Tacitus reports "licentiousness of women was by the senate restrained with severe law." In the case of Vistilia, he relates she was "a lady born of a praetorian family [who] had before the aediles published herself a prostitute." Her punishment was banishment to the Isle of Seriphos.[5]

During this period, the courtesan fell into a miserable state and virtually disappeared. To be seen openly with an avowed courtesan came to be considered a disgrace by the Roman citizen.[6]

Not quite as public-spirited as Solon, but intent on accumulating wealth, Roman owners of female salves continued to employ them in the highly profitable sex trade. Women worked as prostitutes in brothels, inns or public baths. Abandoned baby girls and daughters sold by their parents were raised for this trade. Prostitution was recognized and taxed, and brothels were regarded by some as a respectable investment.[7]

In Plautus's works we are given a picture of the life of the luckless girls forced to live their lives in such service. Generally, because of limited education and skills, these unfortunate creatures were slaves purchased for whoredom at the nearby slave-markets. Slave-traders would establish slave compounds for their miserable merchandise and would prepare them for auction. Bawds, pimps, brothelmasters and other prospective buyers were given license to scrutinize, to touch, and to probe every aspect of their naked bodies. Subjected to these indignities and subsequent defloration, was often the flower of womanhood from all over, for every nation conquered by the Romans helped to swell the slave markets of the Empire.[8]

Unlike the sympathetic treatment afforded them in the Roman comedies of Plautus and Terence, these slaves, once sold for the purpose of prostitution, could look forward to only a bleak, short existence. They had no rights whatsoever since they were simply chattel, subject to whoremaster or bawd, and further subject to the caprices and obliquities of their current sexual partners. If the fates were kind to such a prostitute, and her person appealed to a buyer, she might be purchased, and thus saved from the ravages of disease and death.[9] But since the mortality rate of ordinary slaves belonging to Roman families was between the ages of twenty and twenty-five,[10] the life expectancy for these unfortunates would likely be well below that.

The *vectigal* (tax) on commercial prostitution produced enormous revenues for the emperors of Rome and continued in existence after Christianity officially supplanted paganism.[11] The first Christian emperor, Constantine (reigned A.D. 306-337), according to the historian Zosimus, "imposed an excise of gold and silver upon all those who conducted business enterprises . . . not even the unfortunate courtesans did he let avoid this impost. . . . And when the time arrived scourges and tortures were applied to the bodies of those who, on account of extreme poverty could not pay the fine. What's more, mothers even sold their children as slaves and fathers prostituted their daughters; they were obliged to give the extractors of the tribute money out of the traffic of such things."[12] Theodosius, however, saw fit to abolish the tax on brothels and brothelkeepers but found it more compelling to rigorously tax the whores themselves. While the brothelkeeper was free of taxation, the inmates were not. Heavy fines were imposed on brothelkeepers or on those giving aid or shelter to a whore. Theodosius permitted the existence of prostitution, but none were to act as middlemen or live off the whore.[13]

The Emperor Septimius Severus (reigned A.D. 193-211) made a half-hearted attempt to ban prostitution, as did the Emperor Hadrian (reigned A.D. 117-138) before him. Making an effort to ban mixed public bathing in the hot baths because it abetted prostitution, Hadrian's endeavor proved unsuccessful and Julian the Apostate, who followed him, restored it.[14]

Brothelkeeping from its inception was business—good business—in spite of taxes, bribes to inspectors, corruption, and other harrassments. Whorehouses were a constant, and ever-expanding, since they were too much a part of Roman life ever to be abandoned. All who profited from this enormity found it a veritable necessity, from common slavedealer to important personage.

During the Roman occupation of England, Southwark High Street was the main road in the country, and the route was lined with inns and taverns to service the increasing number of travelers. If such hostelries were short of good beds, or had poor food, there was one commodity they did not lack—whores. Slave girls served a dual purpose: They offered meals during the day and their bodies at night. There were also independent whores, known as *meretrices, ambulantrices* or "night-moths" (*noctiluces*). Twopenny whores were called *diabolares* (two *obols*), and there were some even cheaper; their minimum rates were a farthing.[15]

Located near marketplaces and whorehouses, the Temples of Isis were reputed to be places of assignation for sexual gratification. With worshippers of all ages and both sexes, Isis was basically a woman's goddess. She was the wife of the Egyptian god Osiris, the mother of Horus, and a whore for ten years in Tyre. Her cult, therefore, appealed to both respectable women and to prostitutes. Devotees dedicated to Isis were often identified with erotic behavior and appealed to all classes of women. The worship of Isis persisted in England until 350 A.D.[16]

The essential difference between Byzantine and pagan attitudes toward prostitution was the view of the prostitute herself. Byzantine society generally considered the whore a creature in the "image and likeness of God" and, she was, therefore, deserving of society's pity. During the reign of Emperor Justinian (A.D. 527-565), prostitutes were regarded as the equal of manumitted slaves as far as marriage was concerned. Justinian contended that as long as ex-slaves could become full citizens after gaining their freedom, the same opportunity should be available to the woman who left the life of prostitution.[17] The Emperor himself became the model for this law; he married Theodora, a one-time notorious whore.

Abraham Flexner, in his analysis of Medieval prostitution, concludes that it took two main forms: "resident" whores that were found in ordinary brothels, and "itinerant," that were attached to armies.[18] Emperor Frederick Barbarossa in 1158 promulgated his *Lex Pacis Castrensis* in an attempt to keep his soldiers from camp-following whores. While soldiers who were caught were severely punished, and the women had their noses cut off, Fernando Henriques believes that even such measures were not really effective with an army on the march.[19]

According to Frances and Joseph Gies, prostitution continued to flourish and by the high Middle Ages (1000-1350 A.D.) it was widely regulated by law both in the cities and at rural markets and fairs.[20] Brothels were regarded as an integral part of city life, so much so that prostitutes were at the disposal of visiting notables, at no charge to them. Every palace was equipped with its own bordello, and every royal tour enjoyed the pleasure of its whores. Brothel visits were looked upon as a form of entertainment, comparable to a present-day visit to a night club.[21]

In many places the prostitute was a "marked woman" because of distinctive dress she was compelled to wear. The town of Bristol banned both prostitutes and lepers, while London confined them to certain areas. In Paris they formed their own guild.

In the high Middle Ages, Frances and Joseph Gies state that the whore was considered an irresolute individual, and her behavior was seen as a reflection of her weak female character. Reclassified as "weak" by the people in power, the prostitute's inferior position operated to her advantage in one respect—she was left unmolested in practicing her profession. Heavier penalties were imposed on clients, procurers, and brothelkeepers, a condition which was sharply reversed in the Renaissance. Since prostitutes merited such little worth in the eyes of the law, they also could not inherit property, make legal accusations, or appear in person to answer charges.

During this period, a strong effort was made to abolish prostitution. The eleventh-century emperor, Michael IV, built a beautiful building in Constantinople for all prostitutes who wished to renounce their lifestyle and adopt nuns' habits. He assured them that they need never again fear poverty if they complied. Great numbers of prostitutes thronged to accept his offer.

Another liberal advance made in the Middle Ages favored the whore: Prostitutes who wished to reform could marry. In the twelfth century, the canonist Gratian declared that marriage to a whore who continued her trade was not possible, but a man could marry a whore to reform her.[22]

Nevertheless, in spite of some advances, women and whores remained suspect. For instance, Henriques believes that witchcraft and sex are markedly associated in the medieval mind. It was common for women to confess that they had had sexual intercourse with Satanic creatures. Such sexual adventures always involved extreme pain because of the disproportionate size of the devil's member. To the unwise and credulous, the sexual aspects of witchcraft served to titillate and to spur men to the brothel. Thus, according to the Elizabethan concept of the female, man's lust was formed and inflamed by the insatiable carnal desire of woman. Such a combination is the perfect specious reasoning for the brothel.[23]

Henriques seems to take a dim view of Medieval prostitution. He believes it was due to the general coarseness of the age, the sexual immorality of the upper classes, the uncertainty of the times, the emphasis on war, and to a great extent, to a pervading sense of disease and death. These factors tended to direct men to drown their fears and anxieties in prostitution.[24]

Added to all of these reasons, there still remained a primary factor which slated for failure the eradication of prostitution: Prostitution proved too good a source of income for Church and throne to abandon. Pope Sixtus IV (c. A.D. 1471) became the first pope to license prostitutes and to subject their earnings to an income tax, thus swelling the papal coffers. His successor, Pope Leo X, is reputed to have increased Church revenues by twenty-two thousand gold ducats simply by the sale of licenses.[25]

During this period the Church was responsible for aiding substantially the increase in prostitution. Though it continued to rail against licentiousness and unlawful sex, it now joined the throne in profiting from the illicit business known as "couillage" (concubinage). Though the practice was especially prevalent in the fourteenth and fifteenth centuries, "couillage" actually came into being when celibacy was forced on the priesthood (A.D. 1080). An aspect of "couillage" was the institution of *focarii* or "hearth girls." These *focarii* were also known as concubines—*meretrix foco assideus* (fire-tending whores) who lived in the priests' houses and served them sexually as well. Though technically celibate, priests tended to keep these women. In England, "couillage" was the name given to the licenses required by the priests to keep these women.

Based on a tacit understanding with Archbishop William of Canterbury, Archbishop Thurston of York and all their Suffragan bishops, E. J. Burford notes that in 1129 Henry I agreed to the banning of *focarii*. Very shortly afterward Henry became aware that priests would pay dearly to keep their women. Therefore, Henry deceived the archbishops, and for a price he allowed the priests to go back to their old practice of keeping *focarii*. These revenues helped swell Henry's coffers, and his successors continued this tradition. King John later added a refinement which netted him even more revenue. He seized the *focarii* and then compelled the priests to repurchase their "hearth girls" at outrageous prices. The custom of "couillage" continued unchecked in England until King Henry VIII dissolved the monastries.[26]

A factor which helped to further the crusade against prostitution was the increase of "morbus gallicus," better known as syphilis. It appeared with unabated fury toward the end of the fifteenth century[27] and was reputed to have been brought to

Rome in about 183 B.C. by General Manlius's victorious campaigns in Asia Minor. The great number of Syrian girls who were scooped up as booty and sold on the market were said to be the source of an epidemic of the "filthy disease" which made its appearance by a venereal sore, probably syphilis. This disease, though not as widespread earlier, was evidently causing the Roman army problems, since, in about 150 B.C., it became mandatory for the soldiers to wash the genitals and to bathe regularly. Pliny the Elder (A.D. 23-79) cites the source for this disease as Egypt in his *Natural History* and prefers to credit the "dirty Egyptians" rather than the Romans, with bringing "lichen" or venereal sores to the unsullied shores of Rome.[28] Scott claims the Bible itself seems to credit many with what appears to be venereal infections: David's condition in Psalm 38 lists the afflictions of a syphilitic sufferer; the fifteenth chapter of Leviticus describes another affliction which bears a kinship to gonorrhea; the plague of Baal-peor, citing a death toll of 24,000 Israelites, bears a suspicious resemblance to syphilis.

The introduction of "morbus gallicus" was later credited to Columbus's sailors, who claimed that they had discovered it in America and personally transmitted it to some prostitutes in Barcelona.[29] We may credit the name "syphilis" to a poem published in 1530 by Girolamo Fracastoro called "Syphilis sive Morbus Gallicus," whose hero Syphilus is struck with the disease because of impious acts against Apollo. Syphilus, a Greek shepherd, cures himself with the element Mercury and then is enjoined to devote himself to Diana, the goddess of Chastity.[30]

The medical world knew little about this new scourge; Fenelius (1496-1558) was the first physician to define syphilis and to recognize its contagious qualities. Though European nations had already been subject to this cankerous pestilence, all fought against the distinction of being the source of its origin. It finally fell to the French, since the outbreak of the great epidemic of "morbus gallicus" (the French disease) followed the Italian campaign of Charles VIII of France in 1494-1495. After the army was disbanded, the disease was transported by the soldiers to other countries of Europe and also was soon taken by the Portuguese to the Far East, to India, China, and Japan.[31]

Of course, syphilis continued to rage because it bred in any area pregnant with dirt and overpopulation. Brothels, and those connected with them, were a wellspring for contagion, but filth and unsanitary conditions were not relegated to whorehouses. Much of England lacked proper hygienic conditions, and the impacted filth found in homes and other public places just as certainly helped to increase the contamination.

During the reign of Queen Elizabeth, Scott mentions the first serious attempt was made to treat those infected with venereal disease in England. W. Clowes, surgeon to the Queen, mentions in his writing that England, as well as other European countries, had a proportionate share of this malady, and that over a thousand cases of venereal infection had been treated in St. Bartholomew's Hospital over a period of five years. Treatment in these specialized hospitals in Europe was barbarous. Since the prevailing opinion held that the venereal disease was God's punishment for the sin of man, every patient suffering from the affliction in France was subject to a sound whipping both on entering and leaving the institution.[32]

The epidemic of syphilis toward the end of the fifteenth century, as well as the moral reawakening of the people, condemned the whore to harsh treatment from the authorities. Since whores and brothels helped to spread the disease, the campaign instituted against the prostitute through all of Europe was most savage.[33]

When Henry VIII abolished the stews[34] of Southwark in 1546, which ended England's only experiment in the state provision of brothels, prostitution was, of course, not wiped out. It was merely driven underground. That whoredom was doing well and was very much alive, is apparent from a sermon Hugh Latimer addressed to Edward VI and to the court in 1549:

> O Lord, what whoredom is used now-a-days, . . . how God is dishonoured by whoredom in the city of London doth suffer such whoredom unpunished. . . . A privileged place for whoredom. The lord mayor had nothing to do there, the sheriffs they cannot meddle with it; and the quest they do not inquire of it; . . . and there is no reformation of it.[35]

By Elizabeth's time, it was beginning to emerge again. The persecution of prostitutes remained a custom; apprentices used to channel their frustrations on Shrove Tuesday by rioting and attacking the brothels and the prostitutes.

Thus, in the last half of the sixteenth century we have two major influences affecting the whore: the reaction of the recent plague of syphilis, and the traditional view of lustful sexual experience in general (and non-marital sexual experience in particular) as being evil.

Though prostitutes have existed through much of time, as discussed, they have a unique historical quality in the Renaissance, which the drama reflects. Women are endowed with new characteristics derived from the period in which the dramas are written—qualities of individuality, venturesomeness and independence. The particularity of this time stems from the change in man's outlook. In the Middle Ages, notes Jacob Burckhardt, man saw himself only through some general category. It was in Italy that this concept started to disintegrate and there arose a new sense of objectivity, a critical sense, to which all worldly things became subject. As a result, man's *subjective* side became most important and he became an *individual,* rather than one who responded as a member of a larger classification.[36] It is this historical quality which had a forceful effect on the English Renaissance and which served as a model for the characters of the enterprising prostitutes in Elizabethan and Jacobean comedy.

The harlots are indirectly influenced by the new ideas rampant in the Renaissance, and they seek to raise themselves through prostitution—the only avenue open to the fallen woman in the seventeenth century. Their tale is generally not one of golden chances and business success. Considering the narrow limitations imposed upon this class of women by society, prostitution is often the alternative for survival.

Carried by the current of the new humanism which endorsed selfhood and worldliness, many may have prostituted themselves to reach their higher expectations; however, most women still wanted merely to fulfill the role assigned to them by society and for which they had been trained—that of wife and mother. If despite the female's best efforts this was denied her, or withdrawn from her because she had been seduced, or had lost a father or a husband, the poverty which became her lot also became the primary cause for her sin; embarrassed circumstances rather than lust was the motivating factor. Poverty was an important aspect which led to the increased rise in prostitution in the seventeenth century. In fact, no modern English or American city of comparable size could lay claim to having more prostitution than London. It is important to note that the economic conditions which played no small part in sowing the seeds of capitalism also gave rise to a new class—the enterprising poor.

A good portion of this new class were women. In rural areas women had played an important role in farming and domestic industries. Many were involved in crafts and a large number were in business with their husbands, or even as individual entrepreneurs. If it were a family enterprise, and the husband died, the wife generally continued to run it herself. All women were free to become midwives, dressmakers, milliners and hairdressers. In guilds where cloth work was foremost, women predominated, and so many unmarried women worked at spinning that they became known as "spinsters." With the development of early "capitalism," the woman's role changed and became secondary; women were in an adverse position during this transitional period.

While England grew wealthy and more affluent women could employ servants, there were still hundreds of thousands of poorer women who were caught in a bind and were unable to support themselves. The erosion of the cottage industries, and the daily absence of the male wage earner, had a very damaging effect on the family, especially the women.[37] Thus, given the limited alternatives open to these "enterprising" women, they were forced to resort to selling their bodies to earn a living. Consequently, when Henry VIII became king, the city was overflowing with countless thousands' of women peddling their persons, their one marketable commodity. Some of these who flocked to the city were innocents who were seduced by "city slickers"; many became mistresses; others, responding to the accent on individual enterprise, set up as independent prostitutes; a great number found their way into the ever-expanding brothels.

The malaise of the day in the world of Tudor England was poverty, high prices and unemployment. Tracing the causes of the new poverty, much of the economic difficulty in Henry VIII's reign arose from his profligate expenditures and foolish wars in France which bankrupted his treasury. He sought to refill it by the sale of monastic lands and the debasement of coinage.

Enclosure of land also contributed in some measure to the economic crises which had been going on throughout Tudor times. However, in Henry VIII's reign, the reaction to this was greater, and enclosures were denounced by More and Latimer, as well as other writers and preachers, both Catholic and Protestant.[38] The "swift progress" of enclosure was primarily due to increased population and accompanying high prices.[39] Vagabonds and the poor increased in the sixteenth century; "population increased from 2½ to 4 million people . . . with limited resources" which created unemployment and inflation, affecting the poor drastically. In addition, returning soldiers were now no longer protected by their lords as in feudal times. Instead, they would end up as beggars or were hanged for crimes.[40]

In *Pericles,* when Marina attacks Boult, the pandar, for his profession, his bitter reply indicates the difficulties faced by the returning soldier: "What would you have me do? Go to the wars, would you, where a man may serve seven years for the loss of a leg, and have no money enough in the end to buy him a wooden one?" (IV.vi.180-183).[41] In *Utopia,* More notes that eviction from the land leads to vagrancy and crime.[42]

Another cause of economic problems can be traced directly to land-hunger, as a result of the increased birth rate which healed the ravages of the Black Death. Under the Tudors there was once again a surfeit of labor in proportion to the land available. Land-hunger permitted the landlord to effect changes in rent and in agricultural methods. With inflation rising between 1500-1560, his costs doubled and, in turn, he raised rents. The peasant with the short-term lease was oppressed and had to off-set the immunity enjoyed by other groups.[43]

The age of Henry VIII created a new type of man. Capitalism had given rise to new landlords and a powerful merchant class. With the destruction of the medieval system and the church's loss of power, the new class acclaimed the disintegration of the medieval ethics regarding moneylending on profit margins;

they failed to look with disfavor on the manipulation of men to make money. This class no longer accepted the medieval theology of "just price," nor did it accept and concept that industry and commerce were to be subject to an "ethical standard."[44] It was this changing code of ethics which threatened established mores and helped to create the new class of enterprising poor.

Though men like Latimer and Stubbes decried the poverty that existed, there were none who could view prostitution as an aspect of poverty, and the prostitute as victim. The whore was still regarded as the temptress who enticed and then trapped men in her lascivious net; she was the agent of unbridled lust. Making the male peccant and addressing him as a malefactor—since both shared the same immorality—remained a posture which could gain no ground.

While the plight of the prostitute went unheeded, some attempt was later made to deal with the predicament of the indigent and the poor; the Poor Law was enacted in 1601 to relieve unemployment. Though the purpose of the law was an enlightened attempt to rehabilitate the unemployed by giving them work, it was not successful.[45] Its function was to provide work, but its methods did not take into consideration the personal liberty of the poor. It sent the "unemployable," who was classified as an "idler," to the House of Correction.[46] The worker then received just enough sustenance to maintain existence. A young idler was often forced to become an apprentice to a farmer or tradesman.[47] An obvious consequence of the Poor Law, therefore, was to encourage the enterprising poor to resist the provisions of this law and to risk being thieves, rogues and harlots, rather than to submit to the punitive actions of this act. The necessity for "houses of correction" was endorsed and prescribed by conservative aristocrats as well as puritans. In *The Honest Whore, Part II,* Dekker graphically describes the correction and punishment of the rogues and prostitutes at Bridewell, as well as of the "idlers," which will be discussed in more detail later in this study.

However, even before the advent of the Poor Law, unmarried, unemployed women were subjected to severe treatment. A statute in existence in the fifth year of Elizabeth's reign stated that unmarried, unemployed women between the ages of twelve and forty were subject to forced labor. By the order of "two justices of the peace in the country (or the head officer and two burgesses in the city)" a woman falling into this category could be retained "by the year, week or day" to do any sort of work, and at any wage they deemed acceptable. If she refused, she was committed to prison until such time as she was willing to serve.[48]

Considering this alternative, the punishment for the prostitute—generally a whipping or incarceration in a house of correction—was not unlike the treatment meted out to a poverty-stricken female if she had no family or means of support, or if she had been turned out by her family because she had been seduced. On the positive side, while prostitution in a brothel involved hazards, it would offer the hapless female maintenance, a better home than that of a prisoner or a forced laborer, some police protection, and possibly even the opportunity to rise above her station to become a mistress or a wife. Such an option might appeal to an enterprising young woman far more than the idea of remaining in a house of correction, or as an involuntary servant, with no prospect of ever escaping from this dreary treadmill. Much later, such a view evidently bore fruit for just such a resourceful female as Nell Gwyn, the most popular of King Charles II's many mistresses, who started out as a servant girl in a bawdyhouse. Toadied and truckled to, Nell Gwyn became the symbol of Protestant womanhood, and the play, *The Feigned Courtesan*, was dedicated to her by its author, the impassioned feminist, Aphra Behn.[49]

Still another factor which invited the enterprising poor to reject the"benefits" of the Poor Law was the English system of justice which prevailed during that period. The English police and its judicial system were clumsy, insensitive and accepted injustice as a necessary evil of existence. The police officers were unscientific, untrained and unprofessional, and G. M. Trevelyan informs us that they were not unlike the constables Dogberry and Verges in Shakespeare's *Much Ado About Nothing*.[50] The constable in *A Mad World, My Masters* plays the same foolish, inept role. Due to the inefficiency of the police officers and the lack of money, more often than not, the lawbreaker escaped and was not prosecuted. Consequently, the judicial system simply served to give further encouragement to the enterprising poor to enter the ranks of organized crime.

Not only did the prevailing economic situation and English justice have a marked effect on the harlot, but the advent of puritanism and its narrow concept of married love strongly influenced her position. William Harrington in his book, *Comendacions of Matrymony,* makes very clear the contractual relationship, as well as the purposes for marriage: "To brynge forth chyldren . . . is ye moost pryncypall cause . . . or else secondarly to remedy ayenst synne . . . to avoyde the synne of fornycacyon. . . . Or elles thyrdely for solace and helpe whiche eyther may have of other without the act of flesshely medlynge."[51] The puritans laid the groundwork for a new dignity in the marriage relationship. The social revolution brought increasing importance and assertiveness to the middle classes, and their concepts were reflected in the religious and poetic endorsement of married love. Corroboration of this view is evident in *New Atlantis,* published in 1627. In this work, Francis Bacon discusses laws and customs concerning marriage in his Utopian Bensalem, "the virgin of the world." It is a "chaste nation . . . free from all pollution or foulness." Bensalem's "wise and excellent laws" allow only monogamy and permit no concubines.[52] John Milton, however, one of the greatest puritans, was strongly of the opinion that while a wife is not simply a sexual object, she is less than a man: "Hee for God only, shee for God in him" (*Paradise Lost, IV,* 299).[53]

Early seventeenth-century tightening of sexual attitudes was mainly the work of Protestant, and especially puritan, preachers who strongly emphasized the sanctity of marriage. As a result, the pulpit became more vocal in its opposition to extramarital relations and the double standard. Such denouncements were strongly in accord with the puritan ethic of thrift and hard work; carnality, too, was loathsome.

Both Calvin and Luther sought to instill the spirit of clean living, and if carnal desires were satisfied outside the marriage bed, such deplorable behavior would result in extreme punishment. Sins of the flesh took on a more important aspect in the hierarchy of evil acts, and both Church and state subjected wrong-doers to public shame or physical pain which debased and demeaned.

With the puritan insistence on the sanctity of marriage, a primary target for punishment still remained the harlot. Nina Epton informs us that one English reformer, Philip Stubbes, puritan author of *The Anatomie of Abuses* (1582), would have liked all whores to be cauterized with a red-hot iron on the cheeks, forehead, and other visible parts of the body; he deplored the fact that magistrates closed their eyes to the evils of prostitution.[54]   Brothels were forbidden in London but flourished in licensed stews in Bankside Street, Southwark, close to the palaces of the Bishops of Rochester and Winchester. Winchester had jurisdiction of prostitutional gains, and women inmates were known as "Winchester Geese."[55]   Humphrey, Duke of Gloucester, in *Henry VI. I*, reproaches the Bishop of Winchester for giving whores "indulgences to sin." But according to William D. Alexander, in the houses of the great, apartments were set aside for women who were ostensibly employed to do needlework, but actually were used for sexual promiscuity. He says, "so lost to public decency were all ranks of men, that even the clergy were not ashamed to have inscriptions over the doors of these apartments, signifying the use to which they were appropriated." Gentlemen of means did not take it ill that they were "marshall of the king's whores." The great Cardinal Wolsey had the following Latin inscription over a portion of his palace: "The house of the whores of my lord the Cardinal."[56]

A full-scale attack was then made on prostitution, attributable, in part, to violent outbreaks of syphilis. In London, public bordellos were closed in 1546. In Strassburg, the purveyors of the oldest profession drew up a petition when their establishments were closed down, stating that they were prostitutes not out of love, but out of need to earn a living. Serious reformers attempted to seek a solution. They tried to give the sinners work, but an even better solution, they claimed, "was to get them husbands."[57]   The solution of providing husbands for whores is often used in the comic drama of the period. *A Trick to Catch the Old One* (Middleton), *A Mad World, My Masters* (Middleton), *A Woman Is a Weathercock* (Field), *The Woman Hater* (Beaumont), *Eastward Ho* (Jonson, Chapman, Marston), *Ram-Alley* (Barry), *Northward Ho* (Dekker, Webster) and *The Fleire* (Sharpham), are just a few of the comedies in which the fate of the strumpet is resolved when she is fubbed off in marriage. Possibly due to a feeling that whores were more sinned against than sinning, some legislation was enacted during Queen Elizabeth's time to attempt to protect the prostitute. There may have been a growing feeling that part of the blame for the prostitute's condition should rest on the male. Some of this is apparent in *A Trick to Catch the Old One*. The courtesan addresses herself to her lover Witgood who now plans to abandon her and to marry his virgin: "I have been true to your pleasure; and all your lands/Thrice rack'd was never worth the jewel which/I prodigally gave you, my virginity" (I.i. 36-40). Witgood replies: "Forgive, I do thee wrong/To make thee sin, and then to chide thee for 't" (I.i. 41-42).[58]

In spite of some puritan effort on their behalf, women continued to be victims of the double standard. The suffering imposed on the whore continued unabated since her status, that of outcast, always sinks below that of the "respectable" woman. Examining the inequality of this social force, it is interesting to note that a male is generally accorded greater regard if he is unchaste, whereas just one similar misstep for a woman nullifies an otherwise chaste existence. Bellafront sadly remarks on this in *The Honest Whore, Part I*: "Curst be that minute (for it was no more,/So soone a mayd is chang'd into a Whore/Wherein I first fell" (II.i. 427-429).[59] Once made a whore, it creates almost an insurperable obstacle to marriage. For example, in *Michaelmas Term*, until compelled, Lethe will not marry the Country Wench whom he has seduced. He is, however, willing to act as her bawd. Another common practice which falls in this category is the age-old custom of the rake, rich or poor, to seduce the poor woman and then to marry a rich woman. In *A Trick to Catch the Old One*, this is precisely what occurs. Witgood corrupts the poor girl Jane and then succeeds in marrying the rich virgin Joyce.

Not only are women dupes of the double standard, but of sexual prejudice. Whores, once again, have a high priority as victims of this inequity. Prostitutes are society's scapegoats, whose persecution is justified by rhetoric. Society first subjugates them and then cites their oppressed status as proof of their inferiority. Once this process is set in motion, it develops its own momentum and psychological logic. Women, similarly, continued to be constantly attacked in the sixteenth and seventeenth centuries though the attacks are opposed to the prevailing atmosphere of this period, the more enlightened Renaissance. The continual attack on the whore in this period may have been induced by fear of women. Alexander Leggatt contends that the whore became the embodiment of all evil and her baseness extended to every area. There was not an abomination of which she was not capable.[60] Such vicious representations of whores appear in these dramas: *Green's Tu Quoque* (Cooke), *How a Man May Choose a Good Wife from a Bad* (Anon.), *The Dutch Courtesan* (Marston), and *The Fair Maid of Bristow* (Anon.).

There would seem to be three main attitudes toward the prostitute at this time: Cavalier, Puritan and Liberal. Those dramatists who allied themselves with the more conservative Cavalier position felt no obligation to reclaim the prostitute, nor to despair at the immensity of the task. Punishment—beatings and Bridewell—are accepted, not to reform, but as a concomitant of prostitution. Cavaliers are insensitive to the whore's situation, unconcerned about her ugly existence, and treat her with a large share of disdain. For example, in *Henry IV, Part II,* Falstaff indulges his lecherous tendencies with the whore Doll Tearsheet, while accusing her of carrying venereal disease: "You help to make the disease, Doll. We catch of you, Doll, we catch of you" (II.iv. 44-45). Cuckolding and prostitution were popular themes in Cavalier drama. Ben Jonson has Mistress Littlewit and Mistress Overdo go beyond mere cuckolding in *Bartholomew Fair;* they relish their roles as whores for the short time allotted them. However, the common prostitute, Alice, resents the competition of these "rich one's" who "call away our customers, and lick the fat from us" (IV.v. 65-66).[61] Jonson's view is that the Elizabethan Age reflects the flaws and frailties of the human condition, and he offers no balm to cure its ills.

The Cavalier attitude is exemplified by Dol Common (*The Alchemist*) who portrays a prudent and sagacious lady of sin. Jonson confines her aspirations within the borders of prostitution and makes Dol confident that this is the only avenue in which large satisfactions are available to fallen women. Characteristic of the Cavalier dramatists, Jonson portrays the whore satirically, with high humor, and blandly believed that the sinner was satisfied with her existence. In Dol's case, he felt her life was racy and rewarding and was in no need of reform.

Shakespeare, in common with writers like Jonson and Marston, neither rails nor preaches, and accepts, rather than rejects, the ubiquitous evil of unwholesome sex and whoredom. His generous gesture to help heal an unhealthy condition is laughter—laughter that is not always wholesome or agreeable. While Shakespeare and Jonson generally portray their prostitutes as wrongdoers who whore to survive, and often connive and cheat, seldom are they tarred with the brush of innate malignity and evil. Their grossness and debauchery are concomitants of their bleak, precarious existence, and they are treated with contempt and ridicule. Some of the Cavalier plays which express this point of view are: *A Match at Midnight* (Rowley), *The Coxcomb* (Beaumont and Fletcher), *The Chances* (Fletcher), *The Dutch Courtesan* (Marston), *The Alchemist, Bartholomew Fair, Magnetic Lady, Epicoene* (Jonson); *Measure for Measure, King Henry IV, Parts I and II, Pericles, The Comedy of Errors, All's Well That Ends Well* (Shakespeare); *The Widow's Tears, The Blind Beggar of Alexandria* (Chapman); *The Fawn* (Marston), and *Cupid's Whirligig* (Sharpham).

Those playwrights who associated themselves with the Puritan position were still persuaded that the whore was lascivious, sinful and to be shunned, but there was a care for her reclamation. While the male became accountable in small measure for her condition, he was never held wholly responsible, nor punished commensurately for his part. Puritans did not champion sexual equality; they simply viewed monogamy for both sexes as a more comfortable and pragmatic approach for all involved parties. Puritan playwrights deemed marriage an acceptable solution for the whore's ills, but they demanded total repentance and reform. Despite the rigorous demands made upon the whore to achieve reclamation, the man society allots her, because of her once-soiled state, is a social discard.

The Puritan attitude is exemplified by the prostitute Bellafront (*The Honest Whore*). Heaped high with the guilt of her profession, and obliged to seek survival through her powers of pleasing males sexually, Bellafront is firmly convinced that she is evil. Her love for Hippolito determines her to give up her life of sin. She turns honest and manages to wed her original seducer, who is bitter at being forced to marry his punk. As the wife of Matheo, she is subjected to the tests and temptations of

Patient Griselda, but nothing will induce her to return to her former oppressed state of sin. Puritan dramatists like Dekker attempted to make rigorous repentance, combined with marriage, the resolution for the whore's ills, but the attempt was sometimes foiled by the unhappiness which arose from the marriage. Comedies appropriate to this category are: *The Honest Whore, Parts I and II,* and *The Costly Whore.* Puritan playwrights like Heywood and Dekker treat the harlot as a central character. However, except for *The Costly Whore* (Anon.), there is no other comedy which portrays the harlot as a main character and demands so severe and genuine a repentance as that of Bellafront in *The Honest Whore.*

Though the motivation differed sharply, both zealous Puritan and conservative Cavalier dramatists endorsed punishment for the whore. Puritans sincerely subscribed to Bridewell and beatings because they believed they were a necessary requisite to reclaim the whore; Cavaliers advocated punishment because they supported law and order. Though morality motivated the Puritan concern, an amoral acceptance of the status quo urged the Cavalier course. Thus, the means of opposing ideologies of the moral spectrum are alike, whereas the ends are poles apart.

In addition to the Cavalier and Puritan posture, there is evidence of a middle, or what might be called for the purposes of this study, a Liberal approach to the prostitute which is developed in many of the comedies. The Liberal view is more compassionate than that of the Cavalier and Puritan insofar as it eschews Bridewell, beatings, and rigorous repentance. The cure for the quean's problem generally remains marriage. The Liberal attitude is a realistic one which responds to a less-than-perfect universe and willingly accepts a less-than-perfect solution. The whore who is reclaimed generally marries not her original seducer, but the dubious male whom society feels cannot object to her flawed, frail reputation.

The Liberal view is examplified by Jane (*A Trick to Catch the Old One*). If Jane cherished the idea of marriage to her original seducer Witgood, it is quickly dispelled at the outset of the play. Throughout the comedy, Witgood uses Jane to gain his goals. Because of her imperfect situation and sullied reputation, Jane chooses to comply with his sometimes less-than-moral schemes. In spite of her excellent qualities, she knows that under the double standard, her stigma of sin automatically disqualifies her as a hopeful in the contest to win Witgood. Jane is reconciled to her state, and she prefers to accept the consequences of a flawed universe. She knows that as a courtesan— even a reformed one—society will allot her a less-than-desirable male for a husband. She is, therefore, desperate to marry Old Walkadine Hoard so that she may be made honest. The reclaimed whore knows that marriage is her only opportunity to renounce her unsavory profession and to achieve respectability in a society which never restores the fallen woman to her original position; thus, she accepts her destiny and makes the best of a difficult situation. Some of the comedies which reflect this outlook are: *Ram Alley* (Barry), *Northward Ho* (Dekker and Webster), *Eastward Ho* (Jonson, Chapman, Marston), *The Woman Hater* (Beaumont), *A Mad Couple Well Matched* (Brome), *The Jealous Lovers* (Randolph), *The Knave in Grain New Vamped* ("J. D."), *A Woman is a Weathercock* (Field), *The Fleire* (Sharpham), *Your Five Gallants, Blurt Master Constable, A Trick to Catch the Old One, A Mad World, My Masters* and *Michaelmas Term* (Middleton).

I propose to deal most fully with the following plays which are representative of each of the three views: Cavalier: (Jonson) *The Alchemist, Epicoene, Bartholomew Fair;* (Shakespeare) *Henry IV. Part II, Measure for Measure, Pericles, All's Well That Ends Well;* and (Marston) *The Dutch Courtesan.* Liberal: (Middleton) *A Trick to Catch the Old One, A Mad World, My Masters,* and *Michaelmas Term.* Puritan: (Dekker) *The Honest Whore, Parts I and II.*

However, it is important to point out that the prostitutes in these plays do not always have the same importance in the drama, or are they given the same degree of seriousness or sympathy.

Those dramatists, who chose to depict the whores under discussion as main, or important, characters, may have viewed their literary portraits as "an imitation of life, a mirror of manners and an image of truth"—M. Bradbrook's view of Cicero's definition of comedy—[62] or they may have simply chosen to represent those attitudes which would please their audiences.

Appropriate to this category are those comedies which depict the literary prostitute as a main character, the object of the drama: Bellafront in *The Honest Whore. Parts I and II* (Dekker), and Franceschina in *The Dutch Courtesan* (Marston).

In addition, there is another group of plays which treats the prostitute as an important character rather than as the object of the drama. These portrayals delineate the whore seriously, often sympathetically, and as a fully-rounded individual. Such representations appear in the following comedies: Jane in *A Trick to Catch the Old One* (Middleton), Frank Gullman in *A Mad World, My Masters* (Middleton), the Country Wench in *Michaelmas Term* (Middleton), Dol Common in *The Alchemist* (Jonson), and Dol Tearsheet in *Henry IV. Part II* (Shakespeare).

In *Pericles, Measure for Measure, All's Well That Ends Well* (Shakespeare), *Bartholomew Fair* and *Epicoene* (Jonson), there is no main character of a whore; however, brothels, libertine female behavior, or prostitution have a bearing on the plot and are discussed at some length. Thus, the depiction of prostitution in the plays listed reflects the dramatist's view and his response to the situation.

Historical circumstances, already noted, gave rise to the class of enterprising poor, a spawning ground for the prostitute in the Elizabethan Age. The common quean, and often the courtesan, emerged from this repository and plied her profession, most frequently to escape the stringencies of economic conditions, as well as the inequities of the law, in order to eke out an indifferent existence. Mistress Newcut in *Your Five Gallants,* notes that whores have "but rustical insides and city flesh, the blood of yeomen, and the bum of gentlewomen" (V.i. 27). Others who became harlots, such as Bellafront in *The Honest Whore*, were drawn from good families, educated, and sufficiently venturesome to exploit their inherent advantages when faced with the need to maintain themselves independently.

However, despite social or economic background, in the Elizabethan and Jacobean Age one certainty remained: chastity and constancy were still the bedrock requirements mandatory for women. In the drama, for those who chose not to conform, the punishment in tragedy remained unswerving and severe; in comedy it varied, but erred on the lighter side. In spite of the rigid Renaissance moral code and possibly because of the increased liberality of this period, the attitudes of the playwrights differ from one play to another.

It might be well to observe, however, that though Middleton portrays the courtesan Jane with positive appeal, he tends to have women betray other women; though Shakespeare's whores are often ridiculous and laughable, his Dol Tearsheet is portrayed with sympathy and individuality; Marston makes the Dutch Courtesan pernicious and evil, while chaste Crispinella provides a serious critique of the double-standard marriage. However, Jonson's position seems more consistent; his enterprising women are restrained and cannot rise above their lot; rather, they are defined by it.

Playwrights wrote for both the popular and the coterie theatres. The point of view of the dramatist depends on the writer's persuasion or temperament at the time of composition.

Despite conflicting attitudes toward women—antifeminism vied with the most progressive ethical thinking of the Renaissance—both the enterprising courtesan and the common quean, with their diverse backgrounds, reflect a new bearing in women, a new capacity to venture on their own, and an emergence of personality which strikes a more independent note.

The prostitute's position, however, remained a difficult one. Degradation, the double standard, sexism and stern justice still hounded the whore. Alongside the Protestants' enthusiastic acceptance of married love was the preoccupation with woman's seductive capacities and her tendency to ruin or degrade man. The morality of the Renaissance continued to be concerned with chastity as an absolute, and considering its great value, we can clearly see the fate of the fallen woman in true perspective.

In this period, however, the moral tone is strongly influenced by the humanists. They argued that if society's view of the essence of woman had envisioned her as a temptress and inferior, this view would mold the woman to fit their expectations, and their treatment would reflect this outlook. By the same token, the prostitute's view of herself, based on society's definition of her profession, and the punitive attitudes it adopts toward her, generates or intensifies her sense of worthlessness. The humanists, among other liberals, tended to change society's view of the Renaissance woman by their persistence in destroying some of the old anti-feminist myths, and in their attempt to improve her position. From these changes emerge the independent and venturesome traits which appear in the new Renaissance woman. The reflections of these qualities are mirrored and shine forth in the unconventional person of the prostitute.

The Renaissance whore, now viewed by the dramatist not simply as a low character and a comic buffoon, is often treated seriously, with individuality, and at length in his plays. The Liberal and Puritan playwrights make conscientious efforts to resolve her problem, be it by matrimony or penitence or both. Of interest is the fact that the unorthodoxy of prostitution offers the dramatist one of the few areas in which an independent woman can be presented and treated as a fully developed character, rather than merely as a stereotype. While tragedy deals with larger-than-life heroes and heroines, it is the comedy which serves as a more reliable source for depicting the life of ordinary people. The whore, therefore, offers the comic playwright a better opportunity to examine the sexual morality of the day.

NOTES

[1]See Shackerley Marmion, *Holland's Leaguer*, in *The Dramatic Works of Shackerley Marmion* (New York: B. Blom, 1967), p. 84. Were the term applied to each woman who demanded payment for her labors, it would not only include whores, prostitutes, mistresses and courtesans, but certainly those cases where the wife demands money each time she has sexual relations with her husband. Such an instance occurs in *Holland's Leaguer* (Shackerley), when Millescent, low-born, but virginal, fears her loss of virtue after marriage and wonders what to do with her prospective husband. Her maid, on her wedding morning, gives her this sound advice:

Let him not eat
Nor lie with you, unless he pays the hire
Of a new gown or petticoat.   (V.ii)

[2] George Ryley Scott, *A History of Prostitution* (London: T. Werner Laurie Ltd., 1936), pp. 109, 115.

[3] C. Hayward, *The Courtesan* (London: The Casanova Society, 1923), pp. xxvi-xxvii.

[4] Scott, pp. 76-79. See also Sara Pomeroy, *Goddesses, Whores, Wives, and Slaves* (New York: Schocken Books, 1976), p. 89.

[5] *Works of Tacitus*, Oxford Translation, Rev. *The Annals,* Vol. I (London: Bell and Daldy, 1871), B. ii. 85.

[6] Scott, p. 80.

[7] Pomeroy, pp. 192, 201.

[8] E. J. Burford, *Bawds and Lodgings* (London: Peter Owen, Ltd., 1976), p. 14.

[9] Burford, pp. 14-15.

[10] Pomeroy, p. 194.

[11] Fernando Henriques, *Prostitution in Europe and the Americas,* Vol. II of *Prostitution and Society* (New York: The Citadel Press, 1965), p. 26.

[12] Zosimus: *Historia Nova,* trans. Jas. J. Buchanan and Harold T. Davis (San Antonio: Trinity University Press, 1967), Book II. 37-39, p. 79.

[13] Henriques, p. 26.

[14] Burford, p. 19.

[15] Burford, p. 21.

[16] For a fuller discussion of the cult, see Pomeroy, pp. 217-226.

[17]Vern Bullough, *Sexual Variance in Society and History* (New York: John Wiley & Sons, 1976), p. 325.

[18]Abraham Flexner, *Prostitution in Europe* (Montclair, New Jersey: Patterson Smith, 1969), p. 6.

[19]Henriques, p. 41.

[20]Frances and Joseph Gies, *Women in the Middle Ages* (New York: Thos. Y. Crowell Company, 1978), p. 56.

[21]Scott, pp. 84-85.

[22]Gies, pp. 57-58.

[23]Henriques, pp. 65-66. See also Haselkorn, *Prostitution in Elizabethan and Jacobean Comedy*, p. 91, in which a succubus appears in the shape of Mistress Harebrain, a character in *A Mad World, My Masters,* which seems to support the Elizabethan attitude that women were responsible for male lust.

[24]Henriques, p. 70.

[25]Burford, p. 102.

[26]Burford, pp. 40, 102-103. For the prevalence of this practice, see also *The English Works of John Wyclif,* ed. F. D. Matthews, Early English Text Society, 1880, pp. 35 and 62. Burford lists the editor as F. D. Matten in his "Bibliography and References."

[27]Vern L. Bullough, *The History of Prostitution* (New York: University Books, 1964), p. 133.

[28]Burford, pp. 19-20.

[29]Scott, pp. 143-144.

[30]Henriques, p. 86.

[31]Iwan Bloch, *Sexual Life of our Times,* trans. from the Sixth German ed. by M. Eden Paul (London: Rebman Ltd., 1910 (?)), p. 355.

[32]Scott, pp. 145-148.

[33]*Ibid.*, pp. 87-88.

[34]"Stew" originates from the fact that so many brothels were located in Southwark, known for its pools or ponds, which were used to clean and sweeten live pike and tenches. See Amos Sheldon, *A Comparative Survey of Law in Force for the Prohibition, Regulation, and Licensing of Vice in England and Other Countries* (London: 1877), pp. 516-517.

[35]"Latimer's Third Serman before Edward the Sixth," in *Sermons of Bishop Hugh Latimer*, G. E. Corrie, ed., The Parker Society (Cambridge: The University Press, 1884), p. 196.

[36]Jacob Burckhardt, *The Civilization of the Renaissance in Italy*, II (New York: Harper & Row, 1958), pp. 143-144.

[37]See John McNamara and Suzanne F. Wemple, "Sanctity and Power: The Dual Pursuit of Medieval Women," p. 114, and Richard T. Vann, "Women in Preindustrial Capitalism," pp. 203-205, in *Becoming Visible*, ed. Renata Bridenthal and Claudia Koonz (Boston: Houghton Mifflin Company, 1977).

[38]Thomas More, *Utopia*, ed. Edward Surtz (New Haven: Yale University Press, 1964), p. 26. See also *Sermons of Bishop Hugh Latimer*, pp. 248-249.

[39]*The Tudors*, ed. Joel Hurstfield (New York: St. Martin's Press, 1973), p. 111.

[40]*Elizabethan People: State and Society* (documents), ed. Joel Hurstfield and Alan G. R. Smith (New York: St. Martin's Press, 1972), pp. 28-30.

[41]*Pericles. Works of William Shakespeare*, ed. William Aldis Wright (1891-1893; rpt. New York: AMS Press, 1968). All citations from all the following plays are from this edition by Wright: *Measure for Measure, Henry IV, Parts I and II*, and *All's Well That Ends Well*.

[42]More, p. 25.

[43]G. M. Trevelyan, *English Social History* (New York: David McKay Company, 1965), p. 122.

[44]Douglas Jerrold, *England: Past, Present and Future* (New York: W. W. Norton, 1950), pp. 67, 88.

[45]*Elizabethan People,* p. 59.

[46]Trevelyan, p. 230.

[47]G. M. Trevelyan, *England Under the Stuarts,* 21st ed. rev. (New York: Barnes and Noble, 1957), p. 20.

[48]Carroll Camden, *The Elizabethan Woman* (Houston: The Elsevier Press, 1951), pp. 104-105. Men, too, were forced laborers, but it is interesting to note that there is a special statute applicable to women.

[49]See Bullough, *The History of Prostitution,* pp. 150-151, and Henriques, pp. 108-111.

[50]Trevelyan, *Under the Stuarts,* p. 21.

[51]Chilton Latham Powell, *English Domestic Relations 1487-1653* (New York: Russell and Russell, 1972), pp. 232-233.

[52]Francis Bacon, *Advancement of Learning and New Atlantis* (London: Oxford University Press, 1960), p. 284.

[53]For a discussion of the wife's status in puritanism, see James T. Johnson, *A Society Ordained by God: English Puritan Marriage Doctrine in the First Half of the Seventeenth Century* (Nashville: Abingdon Press, 1970).

[54]Nina Epton, *Love and the English* (Cleveland: World Publishing Company, 1960), p. 91.

[55]Burford, p. 127.

[56]William D. Alexander, *The History of Women,* Vol. I (London: W. Strahan and T. Cadell, 1779), pp. 11-12.

[57]Bullough, *History of Prostitution,* p. 131.

[58]Thomas Middleton, *A Trick to Catch the Old One, Works of Thomas Middleton,* ed. A. H. Bullen (New York: AMS Press Inc., 1964).

All further references are to this edition.

[59]Thomas Dekker, *The Honest Whore, Parts I and II,* ed. Fredson Bowers (Cambridge, 1955). All further references are to this edition.

[60]Alexander Leggatt, *Citizen Comedy in the Age of Shakespeare* (Toronto: University of Toronto Press, 1973), pp. 99-100.

[61]Ben Jonson, *Bartholomew Fair,* ed. Eugene M. Waith (New Haven: Yale University Press, 1963). All further references are to this edition.

[62]M. Bradbrook, *The Growth and Structure of Elizabethan Comedy* (Berkeley: University of California Press, 1956), p. 108.

CHAPTER I

THE CAVALIER VIEW

In opposition to Puritan and Liberal approaches, the Cavalier attitude toward the prostitute was generally "light"—a good-natured cynicism which expected nothing in the way of reform, was uncaring about her condition, and often made the harlot the butt of low comedy. In the Cavalier comedies the portrayal of the punk ranges from that of a foolish female, treated contemptuously or satirically, to one drawn with a larger share of individuality, ambition and pluck. There are many examples of the disdainfully treated whore in the Cavalier drama, such as Sue Short-heels in *A Match at Midnight* (Rowley), Doll in *The Coxcomb* (Beaumont and Fletcher), and Constantia in *The Chances* (Fletcher), but this chapter will generally focus upon the more fully drawn Cavalier portrayals of fallen women in Jonson's *Bartholomew Fair*, *The Alchemist* and *Epicoene*; Shakespeare's *Measure for Measure, Henry IV, Part II, All's Well that Ends Well, Pericles*; and Marston's *The Dutch Courtesan*.

BEN JONSON

The Cavalier vision seems to lie behind Ben Jonson's depiction of the strumpet in his comedies, insofar as she is portrayed as no more immoral—possibly far less—than the married woman who cuckolds her husband and covers her indulgences under the umbrella of marriage. Jonson presents Dol Common, in *The Alchemist*, as an attractive, intelligent, witty prostitute whose profession, nevertheless, destines her to an ignominious existence; whereas respectably married Mrs. Littlewit and Mrs. Overdo, in *Bartholomew Fair*, play at prostitution and their none-the-wiser, cuckolded husbands continue to accord them the due of dutiful wives.

Not all of Jonson's critics agree that his view seems to indicate that the Elizabethan Age is not a pure one and that he does not feel responsible to wipe out wickedness, whoredom and cuckoldry.[1] Though nothing constrains us to categorize Jonson either as puritan moralist or cavalier cynic, if we examine his comic world we see that his rewards always await the wits—Ned Knowell and Welbred in *Every Man in His Humor;* Clerimont and Truewit in *Epicoene;* Lovewit in *The Alchemist;* Quarlous and Winwife in *Bartholomew Fair*--rather than the railers and the preachers. Therefore, to attribute to Jonson the role of reformer would, by the nature of his dramatic precepts, create for him a kinship with the "dogooders" and the deserving. Such an alliance with the morally scrupulous would link Jonson with the righteous, spoilsports like Surly in *The Alchemist,* who wish to recast the mold of creation and who will not suffer venal sin to take its course, a course generally in accord with Jonson's comic resolutions.[2]

The inevitable triumph of the Cavalier viewpoint in Jonson's comedies urges us, therefore, to assume that he accepts the unregenerate world which rejects the morally fastidious and rewards the morally pococurante—wits who sport with fools for gain, but wits who never succumb to punitive motives or willful destruction. Thus, Jonson's Cavalier attitude as it embraces the role of the prostitute in his comedies, highlights his complacent cynicism, a view which does not encourage or expect transformation, a view which lacks the strong sense of obligation and onus of the reformer, but one which makes a world more satisfying for his wits than for his whores.

The Alchemist[3]

While whores and their concomitant ills were pronounced evil by all, the Cavalier dramatists conceded that they were a necessary evil. Many were depicted as garden-variety, lacklustre, one-dimensional figures, but Dol Common in *The Alchemist,* is a most uncommon quean who is characterized as a woman of intelligence, ability and inspiration. She acts the role of a lady with such verisimilitude that it suggests she may have come from an upperclass family. Due to changing economic patterns in the seventeenth century, it was not uncommon for a young woman with a good background to blunder into the realm of sin. Though Dol abounds in ladylike qualities, is canny, clever and resourceful, Jonson's posture is that Dol is satisfied with her role and is convinced that prostitution is the path for her; its rewards parallel her ability.

When called upon to deceive Sir Epicure Mammon—a knight who had wild visions of transforming all of his possessions into gold and silver—about her true status, Dol acts with absolute perfection the educated lady. When the plan is being initiated to gull Mammon and to impress him with her breeding and erudition, Dol informs Subtle and Face that she is well aware of the behavior so necessary to the proper portrayal of the lady: "I'll not forget my race, I warrant you./I'll keep my distance, laugh, and talk aloud;/Have all the tricks of a proud scurvy lady,/And be as rude as her woman" (II.iv. 8-11).[4] She studies alchemy, astrology and mathematics, plays the cittern, and has an avid interest in those scholarly pursuits that deal with nature. Not only is Mammon convinced that Dol is a cultivated lady, but he sees in her beauty a patrician quality. He compares her features to those of the nobles of the house of Valois, the Medici of Florence, and the Austriack princes: "There is a strange nobility i' your eye,/This lip, that chin!" (IV.i. 54-55). With perfect hauteur, Dol replies: "Troth, and I have been lik'ned/To all these princes" (60-61). Mammon, completely captivated, replies: "A certain touch, or air/That sparkles a divinity beyond/An earthly beauty!" (64-66). Since he is assured of Dol's eminence, he feels that her beauty and talent should not be lost to the darkness of scholarly pursuits. Mammon explains that had she been bent, brackish, or ill-formed, such a life might be acceptable, but with her natural gifts, it would be too cruel to live such a cloistered existence. To dramatize his point, he presents her with a diamond ring: "Why, you are like it./You were created lady, for the light!" (108-109). Her excellent acting confirms his belief that "physic and surgery" lie within the province of the constable's wife; she is more fit to be a queen and it is within her realm to enjoy "the air of palaces," "sup pheasants' eggs," and "cockles boil'd in silver shells." Mammon never suspects Dol is a prostitute and is won over completely by her beauty, bearing and intelligence.

Not only does Dol turn her abilities toward captivating
Mammon, a man with a large vision, but with her ability she is
able to satisfy Dapper, a humbler man in a lower station in life,
with limited imaginative horizons. Dol Common's rich creativity
enables her to appear as the Queen of Faerie and Dapper, the
lawyer's clerk, is given an exotic experience which he could not
have achieved through his own impoverished fancy.

Dol's discernment and intelligence are used not only to further the schemes of her cohorts Subtle and Face, but in this
alliance it is largely Dol's ability as peacemaker that keeps the
triumvirate running smoothly. She makes Subtle swear to co-
operate and threatens that if they do not get together and
"cozen kindly, and heartily, and lovingly," she "shall grow
factious too . . . and quit" (I.i. 137-141).

And what is to be Dol's reward for her cleverness and
ability? Subtle bows to her superiority with the compliment:
"Royal Dol!/Spoken like Claridiana and thyself!" (I.i. 175).
Face goes further:

> For which at supper, thou shalt sit in triumph
> And not be styl'd Dol Common, but Dol Proper,
> Dol Singular: the longest cut, at night,
> Shall draw thee for his Dol Particular.   (I.i. 176-179)

Dol's portrayal seems to signify her satisfaction with her lifestyle and her profession. But when we examine Face and Subtle's attempts to commend her actions, it is apparent that they
use an unusual form of flattery. Face calls her "Dol Proper,"
"Dol Singular," and "Dol Particular." Subtle applauds her by
calling her "Claridiana," who is "the heroine of the famous ro-
mance, *The Mirror of Knighthood.*" Such silken blandishments
might serve as a clue. Even among social lepers such as Dol,
respectability, a product of society's expectations, appears as a
desirable, yet unattainable, norm. Her partners' paeans of praise
may be a projection of Dol's unexpressed ambivalence—her satisfaction with her status, and her desire to be both proper and
singular, rather than common. But Jonson laughingly lays the
complexities to rest and resolves all by making Dol a "particular"
prostitute, unique and in demand, but ever the whore, for Dol
is expected also to pleasure her cohorts—Subtle and Face are to

draw that night for Dol "Particular."[5]

Dol, the prostitute, may have consciously or unconsciously flirted with conflicting feelings about respectability, but her view of the widow—an example of the woman who has been married and will remarry—harbored no such ambiguity. When asked how she likes Dame Pliant, her reply is: "A good dull innocent" (V.iv. 68). Dol's belief is that the widow, who exists only as a woman to be married, is stupid and plodding and merits only her condescension.

Dol's opinion of the widow seems justified, considering Dame Pliant's characterization. She is a subservient, submissive female who is made to appear even more foolish than her doltish brother Kastril who decides whom she shall marry. When the widow is manipulated for Face and Subtle's roguish schemes, her brother gives the orders to Dame Pliant: "God's lid, you shall love him, or I'll kick you" (IV.iv. 34). Her meek reply is: "Why,/ I'll do as you will ha' me, Brother" (IV.iv. 35-36). The basis for such characterization is rooted in reality. Succeeding the father, the brother becomes the authority figure for widowed or unwed sisters since women were unable to govern their own lives. Because of their position in society, either father, husband or brother was able to dictate to women the terms of their existence.

Dame Pliant exemplifies the kind of situation which prevailed and is indicative of how women were perceived. Of all women, the widow, generally, was in the best financial position because she was permitted to inherit and control one-third of her deceased husband's wealth. However, she was so conditioned that she, too, turned to the male for guidance. Dame Pliant's situation, therefore, mirrors the attitudes of the age: the acceptance of the conventions is reflected in Jonson's portrayal of the character. Such toleration of the status quo prevails toward all in *The Alchemist,* and in Jonson's comedy the aristocratic cavalier bests the "do-gooder," the mediocre and the mundane. This seems to be borne out in the final scene which finds Mammon cheated, Surly foiled, the other dupes penniless, Face partially vindicated by his wit, and Lovewit winding up with the money, the goods, and the widow. But does he deserve them? Has he earned them? It does not matter, for the verdict on which the play comes to rest is an exhaltation of the roguery of the clever gallant above self-righteous virtue.

Jonson's pungent pleasure in his trickster's cozenage is not misted by ambivalent morality; the cynicism persists to the very end.   If we take this as a summing up of the human condition, there is less value in virtue than in wit, if the wit be male. Even in *The Alchemist* where justice operates in an irrational universe, it is the clever knave, and never the canny quean, who triumphs.

Bartholomew Fair[6]

In *Bartholomew Fair* Jonson again rewards the wily and the witty; they are the heroes.   The crafty all want to make money through the use of their wit. Unlike the fools, they are intelligent; unlike the righteous, they are not morally scrupulous. These characters are represented not in the shallow, savage, irrational world of *The Alchemist,* but in a better, though still somewhat topsy-turvy world.   The prostitutes are tolerated and the cuckolding city wives escape without punishment because they conceal their behavior from their husbands.

Jonson sets the tone of *Bartholomew Fair* in the introduction when the Stage-keeper says: "Would not a fine pump upon the state ha' done well for a property now? And a punk set under upon her head, with her stern upward, and ha' been sous'd by my witty young masters o' the Inns o' Court?" (The Induction, 28-31).   Prostitution serves well as the symbol of corruption and immorality in the play.   Shortly after, we are introduced to Ursula, the bawd and purveyor of roast pig, and Knockum, the disreputable horse trader, who describes the situation to Quarlous: "This is old Urs'la's mansion—How like you her bower? Here you may ha' your punk and your pig in state, sir, both piping hot" (II.v. 38-40).   And Ursula, large, fat and greasy, laughs goodnaturedly at her tormentors when they tease her about her girth and profession: "Aye, ay gamesters; mock a plain, plump, soft wench o' the suburbs, do because she's juicy and wholesome" (II.v 77-78). Ursula reigns the unparalleled bawd, symbolizing the fair—flesh and venality—the world in microcosm. But she is supporter and sympathizer to those who do not deny their frailties, a corollary of the human condition.

Preoccupied with the profits of the brothel over which she presides, and aware that there is a shortage of whores at the Fair, Ursula entreats Whit and Knockum to convince Mrs. Littlewit and Mrs. Overdo to join the daughters of the game, at least temporarily. She pleads: "We are undone for want of fowl i' the Fair here. . . . Persuade this between you two, to become a bird o' the game, . . ." (IV.v. 14-17). Jonson adeptly demonstrates how these middle-class wives not only cuckold their husbands, but, when they play whore, they relish their roles.

Knockum tells Mrs. Littlewit, "It is the vapor of spirit in the wife to cuckold nowadays, as it is the vapor of fashion in the husband not to suspect" (IV.v. 45-47). Mrs. Littlewit is quickly convinced by Whit that the honest woman's life "is a scurvy dull life, indeed" (IV.v. 28), and she quickly realizes that she can live the life of a lady, have beautiful clothes, see plays, be in love with gallants, and all at no cost to her. Her reaction underscores her grasp of the new possibilities, as well as her astonishment at her former naive state: "Lord, what a fool have I been!" (IV.v. 49). Knockum has Ursula outfit both women with the uniform of their profession: green gowns, crimson petticoats, "green" to indicate unchaste women. Ursula is delighted with these "guests o' the game, true bred" (IV.v. 89). After Mrs. Littlewit has already played whore, Edgeworth, a cutpurse, inquires of her if this is not a superior life to that of being saddled with a husband. And her response is, "Yes, a great deal" (V.iv. 60).

But the common punk, Alice, resents the competition of these "rich ones" who "call away our customers, and lick the fat from us" (IV.v. 65-66). Unlike Mrs. Littlewit and Mrs. Overdo, who play at prostitution, Alice, the commercial sexual purveyor, cannot operate from their vantage point; she must work at whoring and must be subject to the risks of lawbreaking and punishment. When Alice complains, Ursula, the bawd, acquaints us with the English system of justice: "You know where you were taw'd lately, both lashed and slashed you were in Bridewell" (IV.v. 73-74). Alice earlier made it clear that Ursula "rid that week, and broke out the bottom o' the cart" (IV.vi. 75-76)—a punishment reserved for whores. In his treatment of Alice, the garden-variety whore, Jonson seems to be more tolerant. However, there remains the sharp touch of reality to remind the audience that the whore is still an evil and must be punished with beatings and imprisonment at Bridewell.

While *The Alchemist* places a mirror to society and reflects its corruption, *Bartholomew Fair* presents an ideal and shows a more humane form of life. Unlike the irrational values in *The Al-chemist*, *Bartholomew Fair* is more charitable and just than the real world, and it would be to the advantage of the world to be mad in this more compassionate way. Thus, Dame Purecraft, crafty cozener that she is, wishes to marry a mad man, and Quarl-ous wins her when he pretends madness. She recognizes that the mad man retains his integrity: "The world is mad in error, but he is mad in truth. I love him o' the sudden . . . and shall love him more and more. How well it becomes a man to be mad in truth!" (V,vi. 157-160).

Even Grace Wellborn, principled and "well born," is subject to the vagaries of a mad world, and it is only by chance, and by the random selection of the madman Troubleall that Winwife, rather than Quarlous, wins her as his wife. But the Fair is a comic world, not subject to the real world of accidents. In such a re-versed universe, we can trust in destiny. Therefore, Grace decides that both Quarlous and Winwife are reasonable and understand-ing, and if fate gives her such a one, she is sure that her own hon-or and rectitude will result in his moral excellence; thus making him the right choice. Moreover, Grace demonstrates her princi-ples and her integrity when she discourages them from harmful competition. Instead, she promises to compensate the suitor who loses.

Quarlous, the wit, loses Grace but unhesitatingly takes his fortune from Dame Purecraft. He accepts what fortune offers him: "It is money that I want; why should I not marry the money, when 't is offered me?" (V.ii. 74-75). Quarlous who ap-pears to be the spokesman for the values of *Bartholomew Fair*, personified in its mad world, testifies to Jonson's Cavalier code—he implies that we must take what we can get without being too morally fastidious.

While Jonson continues to reflect the attitudes and behavior of his age and not to despair at the mass of existing inequities, most critics will agree that Jonson's compilation of female abuse, particularly in *Epicoene*, was largely satirical and that much of it was exaggerated. During this period, little condemnation of wo-men appeared in the plays. However, misogynistic characters mouthed statements which were sufficiently strong so that they led to an unfavorable view of women. While wholesale castiga-tion of women was now a questionable practice, villifying prostitutes was not considered wrong; in fact, such abuse was an indication of the disparager's high sense of ethics. Thus, it is important to examine Jonson's attitudes toward women and, however exaggerated, to realize that they are the touchstone for his treatment of the prostitutes and cuckolding wives in his comedies. It is interesting to note that to those women who wish to move out of their fixed position, Jonson attributes "whorish" qualities, which is a way of subordinating women and making them powerless.

Epicoene[7]

In *Epicoene,* Jonson is unusually harsh in his condemnation of the "learned lady" who chooses to defy the establishment. Truewit describes the Collegiate Ladies as "an order between courtiers and country madams, that live from their husbands and give entertainment to all the Wits and Braveries o' the time, as they call 'em, cry down or up what they like to dislike in a brain or a fashion with most masculine or rather hermaphroditical authority, and every day gain to their college some new probationer" (I.i. 70-77).[8] Truewit's acerbic comments seem directed at women with masculine qualities, particularly since they are bold enough to criticize men in an age when such authority to rebuke was vested in men only.

In spite of attributing masculine qualities to these ladies, Jonson has all of them trying to act as whores. Each, in turn, approaches Dauphine to have sex with him. Haughty says: "My chamber, sir, my page shall show you . . . I pray you wear this jewel for my sake, Sir Dauphine" (V.ii. 18-22).

Centaur also approaches Dauphine for his favors and discredits her rivals Haughty and Mavis in the process: "Good Sir Dauphine, do not trust Haughty. . . . Besides, her physicians give her out to be none o' the clearest. . . . If you'll come to my chamber one o' these mornings early, or late in an evening, I'll tell you more" (V.ii. 26-34). Centaur implies Haughty may have a venereal disease.

Mavis tries to lure Dauphine by pretending that she will "enter into a fame of taking physic" and she will "continue it four or five days or longer," depending upon Dauphine's "visitation" (V.ii. 55-56).

Thus, each of the learned ladies attempts to lure Dauphine and to play the whore. The Collegiates betray not only other women but behave in a manner commonly associated with the dissolute male. They seem to be precursors of the Restoration drama—sophisticated, sensual and libertine. Their attitudes are apparent by their conversations.

Haughty opts for the single standard: "Why should women deny their favors to men? Are they the poorer or the worse?" (IV.iii. 31-32). Haughty and Mavis know that time for play passes quickly and choose a "carpe diem" approach. Haughty believes "ladies should be mindful of the approach of age and let no time want his due use. The best of our days pass first" (IV.iii. 37-38). Mavis says: "We are rivers that cannot be called back, madam: she that now excludes her lovers may live to lie a forsaken beldame in a frozen bed" (IV.iii. 39-41).

Aware that large families rob women of their youth, Haughty practices birth control: "How should we maintain our youth and beauty else? Many births of a woman make her old, as many crops make the earth barren" (IV.iii. 53-55). The practice of birth control categorizes them as resistors of their motherhood role; in turn, this subjects them to the criticism of being "hermaphroditical" or less feminine. Jonson attempts to discredit these women largely because they have stepped beyond the bounds of prescribed feminine behavior. Truewit, totally castigating, sums up their behavior: He finds them uninformed, illogical, scatterbrained, and imitative, and left to their own devices, they have a natural bent for the worst.

Truewit's jibes are also directed at women's chastity, or the lack of it: "Alas, sir, do you ever think to find a chaste wife in these times? . . . I'll tell you, sir the monstrous hazards you shall run with a wife" (II.ii. 27-35). After this prologue, Truewit continues to smear women for the next ninety-five lines in which he accuses ugly wives of domination, beautiful ones of coquettishness, learned ones of wishing intellectual diversions, plus assorted accusations against liberated women, religious fanatics and constant admonitions concerning female unfaithfulness. When Clerimont is inclined to "beware of force" to overcome a woman, Truewit sharply disagrees. When a woman protests such harsh advances, Truewit attributes it to mere posture and deception; her relief at cessation of such abuse is simply another indication of her hypocrisy. Later, in the same act, he pronounces that a woman is simply a sex object, and her sole purpose is to serve man's needs.

Such sharp satire, while exaggerated, is hostile and it tends to degrade the woman and ultimately to further debase the prostitute.

If we examine Jonson's treatment of Mistress Littlewit and Mistress Overdo in *Bartholomew Fair* with that of the "learned ladies," we can discern that Jonson is making a connection between them. In a symbolic and overt way, Littlewit and Overdo actually play at being whores. In *Epicoene,* however, the ladies are portrayed more subtly. There is no indication that they commit the deed, or wish payment, but based on what Truewit says, Jonson is treating them as playing the whore's role—they are acting in a whorish manner.

Jonson attacks and satirizes those women who opt for social mobility, or strain at the moral restrictions imposed upon them, or wish to find freedom by an assertion of selfhood. Middle-class Mistress Littlewit and Mistress Overdo long for the life of a lady; the Collegiate Ladies choose to cultivate wit and learning and to adopt a freer lifestyle; Dol Common desires to profit by her wit and inventiveness. Such unconventional, enterprising women are so locked into their lives by numbing restraints that they cannot actively explore the world, expand their horizons, or rise above their lot; rather, they are defined by it. Instead of equating these women with his wits and gallants—for they are as enterprising and as morally casual—Jonson tends to make or regard them as whores which indicates a certain sexist attitude. Such a view toward these females further condemns the prostitute to an indefensible position and makes the assumption that she is incapable of redemption and must bow to the inequities of her lot.

Thus, if we attempt to analyze Jonson's views, as presented in his comedies, it becomes clear that despite his sharp satire which emerges in his denunciation of fools and women, evident in *Epicoene;* despite his savage kicks at the hypocrisy of the

system and the irrationality of the Order, manifest in his play
The Alchemist; and despite his more genial, just, and
accepting stance, apparent in his play *Bartholomew Fair,*
we can conclude that Jonson was neither zealous reformer
nor insistent moralist. As a Cavalier dramatist, he accepted
the unregenerate world in much the manner of his conservative
wits who opposed changing the established order, an order which
served their needs well.

WILLIAM SHAKESPEARE

Shakespeare, not unlike Jonson, exhibits the same Cavalier
attitude toward the established order and toward the whore
in his comedies under discussion. His belief, too, is that the
Elizabethan Age is not a pure one; he shows no inclination to repudiate prostitution; he shows no repugnance toward the irrefutable evils of this day; he does not propose to
reform. Alfred Harbage, on the other hand, is identifying
Shakespeare with dramas performed in popular theatre
makes this point: "Although both bodies of drama [popular
and coterie] endorse chastity, only the popular plays are
chaste. . . . The others are 'sexy'. . . ."[9] Nevertheless, there
are some conspicuous instances of sexual license which
occur in Shakespeare's "popular" plays: Governor Lysimachus's
regular visits to the brothel in *Pericles;* Bertram's attempted
seduction of Diana in *All's Well That Ends Well;* and
Prince Hal's relations with the whore Dol Tearsheet in
Henry IV, Part II. Though Harbage notes that "Prince Hal
likes 'a pretty wench. . .' ",[10] he maintains that Shakespeare "is silent on the matter" of Henry's "escapades."[11]
But Shakespeare is not totally silent. Just prior to sleeping
with Doll Tearsheet, Hal comments to his companion Poins:
"This Doll Tearsheet should be some road [harlot] " (II.ii.
160). And Poins, to confirm Doll's professionalism, replies:
"I warrant you, as common as the way between Saint
Alban's and London" (II.ii. 161-162). Harbage observes that
Shakespeare saves lecherous tendencies for "clowns." While
he often portrays the common whore in the company of either
his more vulgar characters or his "clowns," Shakespeare's
drama is generally no less bawdy or "sexy" than that of

other Cavalier dramatists.

That Shakespeare's drama neither rails nor withdraws from Elizabethan society but reflects and accepts a less-than-ideal universe would accord with A. C. Bradley's contention that in his plays we do not find " 'poetic justice'— an assignment of amounts of happiness and misery . . . in proportion to merit."[12] Based on Bradley's belief, we might be justified in the assumption that Shakespeare's moral order does not emerge as a strict accounting of justice with rewards meted out to the virtuous and punishment to the evil-doers; rather it is one that would tend to accept the inequities of existence. Bradley believes that "Shakespeare was not attempting to justify the ways of God to men,"[13] a contention which finds rapprochement with "the way of the world" vision and is endorsed by the Cavalier playwrights.

If we examine the role of the whore in Shakespeare's comic world, it would seem to have much in common with this view. Shakespeare concedes the necessary evil of immoral sex and prostitution; he does not protest the lot, or wish to reform the whore; his magnanimous resolution is laughter, which is not always healthy and pleasant.

Henry IV, Part II[14]

In *Henry IV, Part I*, Mistress Quickly is the hostess of the tavern in Eastcheap, a widow who has probably graduated from prostitute to bawd with increasing age and waning charms. Such enterprise by the aging prostitute is generally not frowned upon by the Cavalier dramatist. Her promotion within the trade is recognized as acceptable social mobility. Mrs. Quickly, a comic character, is portrayed as foolish, naive and rather kind-hearted. Falstaff maligns her and Prince Hal laughs at her. Falstaff's contempt is apparent from his conversation with her: "There's no more faith in thee than in a stew'd prune; nor more truth in thee than in a drawn fox; and for womanhood, Maid Marion may be the deputy's wife of the ward to thee. Go, you thing, go"

(III.iii. 112-115). Her credibility, or lack of it, is immediately established, and the marked derision is obvious—she is referred to as a "thing." This conversation is then followed by the usual joking and sexual metaphors. "Why, she's neither fish nor flesh; a man knows not where to have her" (III.iii. 127-128)—all of which stress the low esteem in which the character is held. Thus, to classify a woman as a prostitute is not simply to signify a variant form of personal behavior, but the set of conditions, character, and intent of the classification degrades her, and this reframes her into a non-person, a "thing."

In *Henry IV, Part II,* we meet with Mrs. Quickly again, with a continuation of the same bawdy talk, and with emphasis on her foolish amiability. Falstaff borrows money from her, sleeps with her, and does not pay her. The more compassionate Lord Chief Justice accuses Falstaff of having used the body and purse of this rather good-natured, gullible female. Pressured by Prince Hal's imminent appearance, and promised by Quickly that the prostitute, Doll Tearsheet, will ready herself for the Prince's visit, Falstaff is prodded into making a dubious commitment to pay some of the debt. Unlike Hostess Quickly, Doll Tearsheet bears a closer kinship to Dol Common, for she is enterprising. This is reflected in the selection of her clients. Approached by the disreputable Pistol who wants to avail himself of her services, she says: "I scorn you, scurvy companion. What! you poor, base, rascally, cheating, lack-linen mate! Away, you mouldy rogue, away! I am meat for your master" (II.iv. 115-118). Dol is ambitious; she prefers Prince Hal to Pistol.

Pistol, swaggering as a newly-appointed captain, arouses only Doll's scorn. When he persists in harassing her, she calls him a "cut-purse" and "bottle-ale rascal" (II.iv.) and verbalizes her contempt for his new status: "You a captain! you slave, for what? For tearing a poor whore's ruff in a bawdy-house?" (II.iv. 134-136). Stung by Doll's abuse, the knave Pistol rants that he could tear her apart and will seek his revenge. Grateful to Falstaff for driving Pistol out, Doll cries: "Ah, you sweet rogue, you! . . . Ah, rogue! i'faith, I love thee. Thou art as valorous as Hector of Troy, worth five of Agamemnon, and ten times better than the Nine Worthies" (II.iv. 206-210). Though a whore, Doll is kind, quick and has some knowledge of the classics and the Bible. How does Doll propose to express her gratitude to Falstaff? She offers him her most marketable commodity, her body: "I'll canvass thee between a pair of sheets" (II.iv. 215).

Though Falstaff shows his "gallantry" toward Doll by driving Pistol away (he cares little for him anyway), his attitude toward her soon takes on its accustomed mien and he taunts her, accusing her of spreading the disease of her occupation, syphilis: "You make fat rascals, Mistress Dol" (II.iv. 41). And Dol sharply rebukes him: "I make them? Gluttony and diseases make them; I make them not" (42-43). But Falstaff insists: "If the cook help to make the gluttony, you help to make the diseases, Doll: we catch of you, Doll, we catch of you; grant that, my poor virtue, grant that" (II.iv. 44-46). In spite of Falstaff's accusations and condescending banter, Doll shows sympathy and warmth toward him. When he is off to the wars, she is genuinely touched: "I cannot speak; if my heart be not ready to burst,—well, sweet Jack, have a care of thyself" (II.iv. 366-367). Doll, however, cannot indulge herself for long in such tender sensibilities, for as Falstaff leaves, Bardolph calls for her to pleasure the Prince. And our Hostess blubbers: "O, run, Doll, run; . . ." (II.iv. 376).

Though Mrs. Quickly, as bawd, and Doll Tearsheet, as whore, have ministered to Prince Hal's wants, they remain legal and social castoffs, and they must expect to take their punishment. The royal client does not intercede in their behalf. They are delivered over to the Beadle and they will be whipped. Doll, attempting to escape the punishment, pugnaciously pleads pregnancy. But the Beadles will not be deceived by this ruse and are contemptuous of her attempt to simulate pregnancy.

Ironically, Doll's words to the Beadle are: "Bring me to a justice" (V.iv. 26), but she knows that the Beadle will see to it that the justice meted out to her will be that "she shall have whipping-cheer enough" (V.iv. 5). Though both women rail against the injustice of the situation, the audience will be expected to respond with light laughter and mild cynicism. Whores are powerless, and the play reflects their condition. Society demands punishment for these "moral defectives," and at the end of the comedy Bridewell awaits them, the traditional treatment awarded these women. The degradation in which the prostitute is held, the punitive attitude society adopts toward her, are but reflections of an age which attaches great penalties to a promiscuity in women it does not think to punish in men.

In presenting his less-than-ideal universe, Shakespeare accepts the institution of prostitution and the existence of whorehouses as very much a part of life. In *Measure for Measure*, whorehouses exist both at the beginning and at the end of the play. When Lord Escalus tells Pompey that the law will not allow prostitution, the clown cynically replies: "Does your worship mean to geld and splay all the youth of this city?" (II.i. 218-219). Lechery is such a commonplace that when the Duke intends to cure it, Lucio's reply is: "Yes . . . the vice is of a great kindred . . . but it is impossible to extirp it quite, till eating and drinking be put down" (III.ii. 94-96). "Ever your fresh whore and your powder'd bawd; an unshunned consequence; it must be so" (III.ii. 55-56).

Measure for Measure[15]

Prostitution makes its debut early in *Measure for Measure*, when Lucio discourses feelingly with a gentleman about syphilis and its painful effects. As the bawd, Mrs. Overdone, a replica of Mrs. Quickly, appears, Lucio proclaims: "Behold, behold where Madam Mitigation comes! I have purchas'd . . . many diseases under her roof. . . .—" (I.ii. 43-45). Shortly after, the bawd regales us with the problems of her profession. Mrs. Overdone's clientele is rapidly being depleted by the war, the plague, the gallows and poverty. Added to these disasters, the law threatens to close all houses in the suburbs. Not unlike the whores of Strassburg, who drew up a petition when their establishments were closed down stating that they were in business not out of love, but out of a need to learn a living, Mrs. Overdone wonders what will become of her. However, when the law forces the bawd Overdone to move from the suburbs, she does the only thing she knows—she opens a "hot-house"—ostensibly a bathing place but commonly used for brothels as even Elbow, the simple constable, seems to know when explaining the role of the tapster to Angelo: He is "one that serves a bad woman: whose house, sir, was, as they say, pluck'd down in the suburbs; and now she professes a hothouse, which, I think, is a very ill house too" (II.i. 61-64).

Shakespeare strikes a realistic note when he has incompetents such as Elbow staff the judicial system; such inefficient help was due to the poor pay. When Lord Escalus inquires of Elbow why he has had to serve seven years and why there is such a dearth of men to work in this capacity, his reply is: "Faith, sir, few of any wit in such matters: as they are chosen, they are glad to choose me for them; I do it for some piece of money. . ." (II.i. 255-257).

Measure for Measure is a "problem"[16] comedy rather than a joyful one. Similarly, the punishment assigned to the bawds and whores is greeted with less laughter, and the tone, somewhat harsher, is in greater agreement with that of the Puritan dramatist's. While the Puritan's more stringent approach may have been intent on reform and the Cavalier's simply on the preservation of the status quo, the result for the social outcast was the same. Both endorsed punishment. Mrs. Overdone is whisked off to prison, and Pompey, the bawd, is punished in a similar manner by the Duke: "Take him to prison, Officer./Correction and instruction must both work/Ere this rude beast will profit" (III.ii. 28-30). The idea of "correction and instruction" seems to imply a measure of reform which is generally absent from the Cavalier comedies.

But while the fate of the bawd and the ordinary prostitute was an accepted convention, loss of chastity often presented difficulties for the indiscreet maiden. When Isabella learns that her cousin Juliet is with child by her brother Claudio, she appears to be quite unperturbed about the situation and says, "O, let him marry her" (I.iv. 48). Apparently, since Claudio and Juliet were betrothed, even secretly, it was a valid marriage contract, and sexual relations were, therefore, permissible.[17] For someone as morally pure as Isabella, her reply would tend to confirm this opinion. Similarly, based on a pre-contract between Angelo and Mariana, the Duke makes arrangements for Isabella to help Mariana, Angelo's betrothed, insure the success of the "bed-trick." The Duke clearly informs Mariana: "He is your husband on a pre-contract:/To bring you thus together, 'tis no sin" (IV.i. 70-71). It is under these conditions that Isabella agrees to the deception.

When persuading Isabella to help, the Duke is aware that Angelo left Mariana after "she should this Angelo have married; was affianced to her [by] oath, and the nuptial appointed; . . . this well-seeming Angelo" (III.i. 208-217). The Duke notes the reason for his actions: He abrogated his vows because he pretended to discover some dishonor on her part. After Angelo learns that Mariana has been substituted for Isabella, he tells the Duke why he had left Mariana: "Partly for that her promised proportions/Came short of composition; but in chief/For that her reputation was disvalued/In levity" (V.i. 217-220). In this instance, Angelo's displeasure at his financial loss, and the baseless charge that Mariana's "reputation was disvalued in levity," give him the grounds to reject Mariana. However, after the "bed trick," Mariana, like Juliet, is no longer a virgin technically and is subject to the same penalties. In the case of Claudio and Juliet, the double standard is applied by the Duke when he is masquerading as a friar and rebukes Juliet: "Repent you, fair one, of the sin you carry?" She replies: "I do; and bear the shame most patiently" (II.iii. 19-20). Juliet tells the Duke that she loves Claudio and the Duke asks: "So then it seems your most offenceful act/Was mutually committed?" (II.iii. 26-27). Learning that it was mutual, the Duke declares: "Then was your sin of heavier kind than his." And Juliet concedes: "I do confess it, and repent it, father" (II.iii. 29). Though both committed the "offenceful" act, Juliet is held to be more responsible than Claudio.[18]

The marriages of Juliet and Mariana are based on a precontract. *Measure for Measure* seems to argue that both women are not whores, except on the basis of the strict puritan view, represented by Angelo, and which the play is concerned with repudiating.

Angelo, until he falls, is a severe, strict, and unbending moralist, similar to Malheureux in *The Dutch Courtesan,* who is characterized as "a man whose blood/Is very snow-broth, one who never feels the wanton stings and motions of sense" (II.i. 57-59). In Angelo's excessive puritanical zeal, he exhumes a law which has been buried for nineteen years and applies it to cure sin. Caught in the net of this legal tangle, Juliet is labeled a "fornicatress" by Angelo, is imprisoned, and Claudio must face death. Angelo's hypocrisy and his harsh justice, rigid against all pleas of mercy, reflect a puritanical zeal, and at the end, he is exposed.

The Cavalier view, which the play more readily represents, would have accepted the existing order, i.e., to see Juliet and Claudio's act as legal and honest. However, Angelo insists upon importing puritan attitudes—sin is serious and can be cured by sufficient repentence—which, according to him, extends even to death. *Measure for Measure,* nevertheless, is concerned with disavowing this view.

Lucio's marriage to his whore is more in keeping with the Cavalier attitude. His marriage does not fall in the same category as Juliet's and Mariana's since there is no pre-contract. It would also seem that the Duke is not primarily concerned with meting out justice for Lucio's whore. Rather, Lucio's foul lies about the Duke have so inflamed him that punishment of Lucio becomes the Duke's major thrust. Since *Measure for Measure* is classified as a "problem" play which ends happily, the Duke rescinds the punishment of whipping and hanging, but he insists upon Lucio's marriage to the whore. When Lucio pleads that "marrying a punk . . . is pressing to death, whipping, and hanging" (V.i. 520-521), the Duke's reply is, "Slandering a prince deserves it" (522). Such a severe rejoinder leaves little doubt that punishment for Lucio, rather than "caring" for the whore Kate Keepdown, is the Duke's major motivation for the marriage.

Pericles[19]

Prostitution and bordellos, as in *Measure for Measure,* are again a part of the scene in *Pericles.* Venereal disease is always a concomitant ill of the bawdyhouse, and most often attributed to the French. The Bawd says that Mons. Verollus, a client, "brought his disease hither; here he does but repair it" (IV.ii. 111-112). Another reference to the disease occurs when Lysimachus answers Boult, the Pandar's servant: "How now, wholesome iniquity have you that a man may deal withal, and defy the surgeon?" (IV.vi 23-25).

The short supply of "fresh" prostitutes was undoubtedly a common problem for bawds since both Ursula in *Bartholomew Fair* and the bawd in *Pericles* have the same concern. The Pandar is asked to carefully comb the market because Mytilene has so many prospective clients, and the bawd has already taken losses because of a dearth of this commodity. The Pandar is in ready agreement and insists that they have "fresh ones"; the ultimate delicacy in the brothel was the virgin with the maidenhead, preferably an "honest" one not sold over and over.[20] Therefore, Marina's chastity elicits much excitement. The Bawd instructs Boult to get a catalog of her physical characteristics and above all, a warranty that she is a virgin. He is instructed to publicize the fact that the highest bidder will have the opportunity to deflower her. The dogma of chastity being what it was, the bawd knows that the value of such a scarce commodity is highly prized. The bawd, ever the entrepreneur, then brings on the virgin Marina and hawks her merchandise: "Here comes that which grows to the stalk; never pluck'd yet, I can assure you" (IV.vi. 40-41). Lysimachus, evidently pleased, retorts: "Faith, she would serve after a long voyage at sea" (IV.vi. 43-44). Since virginity is a commodity as well as a moral virtue, this ideal state will be maintained regardless of the dangers which must be overcome to keep this prize intact for Marina's lawful husband. When Marina realizes that her "jewel" will be forfeited too soon, and she will fall from innocence into sin, her rejoinder is: "If fires be hot, knives sharp, or waters deep,/Untied I still my virgin knot will keep" (IV.ii. 147-148).

Boult, ever practical, fears that Marina's invincible chastity is bad for business and will drive away their "cavaliers." Though it was expected that Marina would remain unsullied (she is of the royal line and such behavior is in keeping with Degree), such conduct was not required of the male, even the royal male. Quite the contrary, it was expected that Lysimachus, the governor, would not frown on prostitution and would avail himself of its gross pleasures.

After meeting Marina in the brothel, Lysimachus declares that she is "a creature of sale" (IV.vi. 77), and Marina, in her simplicity, quite rightly chides "honorable" Lysimachus: "Do you know this house to be a place of such resort, and will come into 't? I hear say you are of honourable parts, and are the governor of this place" (IV.vi. 78-80). Distrusting Marina, he fears that she wishes to use his high position as a stepping stone for her ambitions, possibly even marriage. Lysimachus, espousing the Cavalier view, expects from Marina a prostitute's performance and cautions her that trickery or deceit to further her aspirations will be thwarted.

But since this is a comedy and due for a happy ending, Shakespeare must bring about the reconciliation of Marina and Lysimachus. One path is for Marina to make manifestly clear to him that she is an honorable virgin and to use her persuasive powers to maintain that enviable state. As long as an untouched maiden (particularly one with persuasive powers and of noble birth) retains her innocence and does not fall, the Cavalier dramatist endorses her power for good; i.e., the ability to turn men away from temptation and sin, which Marina apparently does: She appeals to Lysimachus to set her free, and he becomes suddenly converted by her purity. Marina blesses him and this spurs the new convert on to greater condemnation of anyone who would ravish a virgin: "Thou art a piece of virtue, . . . A curse upon him, die he like a thief,/That robs thee of thy goodness!" (IV.vi. 110-114). "Your house, [Boult] but for this virgin that doth prop it,/Would sink and overwhelm you. Away!" (IV.vi. 118-119).

Irked by Marina's "peevish chastity," which is bad for business, the Bawd instructs Boult to violate her and thus make Marina more malleable. And in obvious satire, the Bawd and Pandar are represented as slighted by the undue stress Marina places on her virginity: "She makes our profession as it were to stink afore the face of the gods" (IV.vi. 134-135). The situation becomes more realistic when the Bawd prods Marina to give up her pose so that she may "go the way of womenkind" (IV.vi. 148). Women betraying women, a classic theme throughout literature, appears in the Renaissance drama.[21] While Marina does not make Boult a believer as a result of her proselytizing, she is able to convince him of her apodictic need to remain chaste. Marina can and will do anything—sing, weave, sew, dance—to remain a virgin. And, of course, in "fairy tales" pure, unstained princesses marry princes (or converted governors) to live happily ever after. But a note of authenticity creeps in when cynical Boult is sure that an ordinary virgin could not have swerved Lysimachus: "The nobleman would have dealt with her like a nobleman" (IV.vi. 137-138) intimating that he would have used her as a whore and would have ignored both her railing and her cries of innocence.

All's Well That Ends Well[2][2]

Not only in *Measure for Measure* and *Pericles* do we observe that chastity is a virtue, but it appears also in *All's Well That Ends Well*. As the play opens, Helena is bantering with Parolles about the difficulties encountered in a maiden's attempt to win her man and to retain her virtue. Despite its value, Parolles reminds Helena that virginity is a marketable commodity which "will lose the gloss with lying; the longer kept, the less worth" (I.i. 143-144)—better to change it for a wife. Diana, Helena's conspirator, is also well-schooled and knows that pre-marital inducements offered in exchange for female virtue by the male are to be shunned. In the marriage marketplace, premarital chastity is a powerful negotiating tool, and if the woman is unwise enough to bargain it away before the contract is signed, she becomes defective merchandise.

But Bertram, anxious to seduce Diana, makes promises that he will love and serve her forever. Her knowing reply confirms her pragmatic upbringing: "Ay, so you serve us/Till we serve you; but when you have our roses,/You barely leave our thorns to prick ourselves,/And mock us with our bareness" (IV.ii. 16-19). And she continues: "Therefore your oaths/Are words and poor conditions, but unseal'd (IV.ii. 29-30). . . . My chastity's the jewel of our house" (IV.ii. 46). Marriage vows are the only acceptable form of barter for the sale of virtue. And circumstances prove that Diana's value of this ideal state is justified. The gratuitous gift of chastity is a fall not only from innocence to sin but from power to impotence. This view is later borne out when Diana appears before the King to demand that Bertram keep his promise to marry her, which occurs before Helena appears to explain the role Diana plays in Bertram's deception. Bertram is, therefore, still under the illusion that he has seduced Diana and he "boggles shrewdly" to free himself from his pledge. Accused of breaking his commitment to her by the King, he maligns her and assumes a superior attitude: "Lay a more noble thought upon mine honour/Than for to think that I would sink it here" (V.iii. 178-179).

Diana, as well as Helena, is his social inferior, and no "gentleman" worth his repuation is above corrupting a young woman, particularly of lower birth. Parolles admits to the King that his master was an honorable gentleman, but he did what all honorable gentlemen feel free to do. Bertram, to disengage himself from his predicament, continues to revile Diana: "She's impudent, my lord,/And was a common gamester to th' camp" (V.iii. 185-186). . . . "I had that which any inferior might/At market-price have bought" (V.iii. 216-217). Inveighing against women and calling them whores is not a new form of invective especially since the pervading attitude during the Renaissance made it a virtue to denounce whores, whereas impugning the female sex was less acceptable.

Though Shakespeare attempts to shelter Bertram and Helena's difficulties under the panoply of an uncertain marriage, he seems constantly to remind us that life hinges on the attitudes and values which society dictates. Such views, particularly as they apply to the female, declare that chastity is an absolute, that constancy is a requirement, and the the double standard of sexual conduct shows the male indulgence that the female cannot hope for. Such attitudes are clearly expressed in the Shakespearean comedies discussed in this chapter. Like Jonson, Shakespeare accepts an imperfect universe and realizes that relentless railing and fanatic preaching neither negate nor affirm established codes and accepted morality. Shakespeare's plays are not pure, nor do they incorporate the strong puritan morality. Rather, he is the more gifted dramatist who, when necessary, pandered to his public. His vision, therefore, pragmatically accepts the reality of the whore as a constant on the Elizabethan scene.

Though Shakespeare's basic attitude is Cavalier, his plays were not totally Cavalier and had sufficient appeal to the middle classes who were more puritanically inclined. There are times in which Shakespeare does approach a more puritanical view. For instance, pronounced puritanical tendencies are evident in *Pericles*. Marina, despite the pressure put on her to become a prostitute, manages to elude this lewd existence, is able to remain chaste, and attempts to reform all immorally tainted characters whom she meets in the brothel. While Shakespeare has some puritanical proclivities, a more representative example of such a predilection among the Cavalier playwright's approach to the prostitute can be seen in Marston.

JOHN MARSTON

The Dutch Courtesan[2 3]

A Cavalier dramatist who is a lesser figure than Jonson and Shakespeare, "Marston [is] one of the most interesting," T. S. Eliot finds, "and least explored of all the Elizabethans—. . ."[2 4] Caught between those who disavow him because of his vituperation, violence and moral posturing, and by those who applaud him because of his serious social satire and strong moral judgments, Marston's critics are strongly polarized. But somewhere between these extremes there seems to exist another appraisal, perhaps more acute, of Marston's vision, particularly as it applies to his comedies.[2 5] In *The Dutch Courtesan* Freevill and Cocledemoy are sophisticated, young gallants. The wits win out and Cocledemoy concludes that whatever has been done has been for wit's sake. Freevill frankly endorses prostitution, and Cocledemoy praises the bawd's profession. Thus, while Marston's early allegiance may have been to dark morality, his evolution is more expressive of the Cavalier vision—acceptance of the real world where gallants gain their ends, and the righteous are rarely rewarded—a view shared by other Cavalier dramatists discussed.

While Marston's mood is one of mirth and merriment, and he absolves frail humanity of its foolishness in *The Dutch Courtesan,* the same generosity appears to be absent in the treatment of his whores, especially Franceschina. The argument of the play—the difference between the love of a courtesan and a wife—conceives of the courtesan as an unredeemable, sensual "object" who appeals to a man's lust, and the wife as a faithful, affectionate female who appeals to the male's "lawful love." In the main plot of the play, Freevill is the gallant and future husband of Beatrice, who tosses his mistress, Franceschina, to his friend, Malheureux, a puritan-like character, who instantly falls in love with her despite his recent diatribe against whores. Even after Franceschina demands the death of Freevill as the price of her love, Malheureux persists in his pursuit of her. Not until she betrays him for the supposed murder of Freevill does he realize his folly. Franceschina's plot is uncovered and she is punished.

In my analysis of the predicament of the literary prostitute, it becomes pathetically clear that as a whore, Franceschina is subject to the humiliation, degradation and double-dealing of the male; she is also thoroughly corrupted by her situation. The Dutch Courtesan's maleficence and spitefulness lurk within her, permeating her like a pervasive scent, an odorous quality which emanates from constant conflict with a hostile society and unrelenting submission to the male. The potential poison is activated when Freevill cavalierly casts her off and turns her over to his friend Malheureux because he plans to shred "away all those weak under-branches/Of base affections and unfruitful heats" (II.i. 6-7)[26]—to legalize his wantonness and to marry the more manageable Beatrice, his betrothed. In a cool, matter-of-fact manner, Freevill flings off Fanceschina, rationalizing, "I loved her with my heart until my soul showed me the imperfection of my body, and placed my affection on a lawful love" (I.ii. 89-91). Examining his hypothesis, it is interesting to note that where formerly he loved with his heart, he now replaces this with "affection" on a "lawful love."

His love for Franceschina, evidently, was not ill-conceived, for judging from Freevill's comments, she is more than the common, garden-variety prostitute.[27] Not only can she entertain—play the lute and sing—but there is a sensitivity and a delicacy to which the wit, Freevill, responds. Cataloging her charms to Malheureux, he says: "She's none of your ramping cannibals that devour man's flesh, nor any of your Curtian gulfs that will never be satisfied until the best thing a man has be thrown into them" (I.ii. 86-89). This comment, which may mirror reality, would tend to refute the Elizabethan assumption that women, generally, and whores, particularly, are wanton and lascivious and can never be sexually appeased. Commenting on Franceschina's charms before he is smitten by her, Malheureux says: "She is a whore, is she not?" (I.ii. 96). And Freevill's indurate response is: "Whore? Fie, whore! You may call her a courtesan, a cockatrice, or . . . a suppository. . . . But, whore! Come, she's your mistress. . ." (I.ii 97-103).[28] Franceschina, still unaware of what awaits her, sings a melancholy tune and entreats Freevill not to remain away long. As he lies, "Believe me, not long" (I.ii. 121), Franceschina adds prophetically: "Sall ick not believe you long?" (I.ii. 122).

Malheureux, dazzled by Franceschina, makes a complete

volte face—he "must love her"—and insists: "Beauty is for use!" (I.ii. 131). Envious of the animals who "have no bawds, no mercenary beds, no politic restraints . . . in whom an inborn heat is not held sin" (II.i. 69-73), Malheureux lashes out against wretched man who calls sex sinful, whereas in all other forms of life, it is considered nature's greatest good. As "a man of snow," he fears that loving a strumpet will damage his image. Malheureux must also fear that he is negating puritan principles by his love for a prostitute. His senseless lust is exposing his health, name, and precious time to destruction by a whore. Puritans held that appeasing one's sexual appetite in this illegitimate manner subjected the individual to damnation and deterioration.

Conflicted about his love for a courtesan, Malheureux is chided by Freevill: "Thou art in love with a courtesan! Why, sir, should we loathe all strumpets, some men should hate their own mothers or sisters. . . . By heaven, I resign her freely; the creature and I must grow off" (II.i. 91-98). Continuing to censure Malheureux in a playful manner about Franceschina, his coarse remarks indicate his regard for the courtesan: "Along, sir to her! She's an arrant strumpet; and a strumpet is a serpigo,[29] venom's gonorrhy to man—things actually possessed! Yet since thou are in love—and again, as good make use of a statue, a body without a soul, a carcass three months dead" (II.i. 130-134).

Freevill's frivolous remarks to Malheureux concerning his qualms about loving a whore are intended to tease Malheureux about his former aversion to the horrors of harlotry. Freevill's suggestion to Malheureux that he think of his strumpet as a statue or a dead body invests her with a fleshless, inanimate, or nonperson status; thus, by this sophistical argument, Malheureux's guilt may more readily be assuaged since he is not making love to a living whore. This discussion then prompts Freevill to reiterate his own philosophy about the difference between a whore and a wife: "They [whores] only sell flesh, no jot affection" (I.i. 137-138). Based on this view of the whore, Freevill's love for Franceschina was always dominated by his conception of her non-person status, for how else could he make such comments about her with blatant insensibility, and then donate her so gratuitously to Malheureux, merely as if she were nothing more than an "object," a "thing?"

Taking leave of a miserable Franceschina, Freevill adds egregious insult to crass egoism by telling her she has "grown a punk rampant" (II.ii. 83), and she retorts harshly that she never again wants to see him because he has made her so miserable. Crushed, she cries out against the deception and domination of men. She berates them for being faithless tyrants and betrayers. In her woe she recognizes her paradoxical position. Franceschina knows that the pleasure men take in this illegitimate relationship paves the way for the prostitute's downfall. And having made her hateful, she says, "You only hates us." Immediately, egotistical, insensitive Malheureux, indifferent to her sensibilities, utters: "Will you lie with me?" (II.ii. 122). Her reply is savagely poignant, and it bespeaks her utter degradation: "O vile man, vat do you tink on me? Do you take me to be a beast, a creature that for sense only will entertain love, and not only for love, love? O brutish abomination!" (II.ii. 126-128). When Malheureux again avows his love for her, Franceschina still fears to commit herself and bemoans the lot of woman: "Sall I, or can I, trust again? O fool,/How natural 'tis for us to be abus'd!" (II.ii 134-135).

Not only is Franceschina beset by unfaithful and insensitive lovers, but even her bawd, upon whom she is dependent, seeks to exploit her. When the Dutch Courtesan chafes at losing Freevill, self-seeking, business-oriented Mary Faugh can only suggest another lover in his stead. And when this remark enrages Franceschina so that she cries: "You ha' brought mine love, mine honor, mine body, all to noting!" (II.ii. 7-8), Faugh reminds her that it was she "who paid the apothecary . . . who redeem'd [her] petticoat and mantel" (II.ii. 25-26) and who introduced her to dons, lords, gentlemen and wealthy citizens and tradesmen as clients. The bawd has helped her to her present, more lucrative "custom" instead of to her accustomed "swaggering Ireland captains" and "two-shilling Inns o'Court men" (II.ii. 28-29). Paying Franceschina's apothecary bill implies a bout with venereal disease, especially since Mary Faugh mentions that she has kept the whore's secrets. Franceschina's low-paying clientele may have been responsible for her poor financial condition, and Faugh obliged her by paying the pawnbroker and upgrading her professional contacts. Following this screed, the bawd angrily retorts: "And dost thou defy me, vile creature?" (II.ii. 31).

Then Franceschina's malevolence asserts itself—born of
her profession, nurtured by its indignities, ripened by Freevill's
rejection of her love. The insidious evil, brought to fruition
when she is spurned, manifests itself in her aborted revenge:
"Ick sall be revenged! Do ten tousand hell damn me, ick sall
have the rogue troat cut; and his love, and his friend, and all
his affinity sall smart, sall die, sall hang!" (II.ii. 41-43). Franceschina's plot to incite Malheureux to murder is discovered, and
she is sent off "to the extremest whip and jail!" (V.iii. 59).
Freevill's final damning of Franceschina is, in Cavalier fashion,
generalized to the entire sex: "O thou comely damnation!/Dost
think that vice is not to be withstood?/Oh, what is woman merely made of blood!" (V.iii. 48-50).

Examining Marston's treatment of the whore, it seems to
reflect the Cavalier concept. In his "Prologue" he states that the
purpose of his work "is not to instruct, but to delight," and that
Malheureux's entire dilemma is but "slight" or paltry. His purpose in clarifying Franceschina's "evil" is to reassure the audience that she is not to be taken too seriously—that she is simply
to be regarded as a creature whose "beauty is for use." Her out-
raged feelings which spring from acute anguish are disparaged
by giving her rages a comic twist. All of her intrigues appear
comic because of her accent; a foreign accent signified mirth to
a Jacobean audience. Marston's insensibility interprets the
pernicious plottings of a whore as absurd gestures rather than
overwhelmingly wicked actions. To have dignified Franceschina's problem with a serious rather than a comic approach
would have been an augury of concern or interest in the whore's
problem. But Marston shows no inclination to move in this
direction.

Not only does Marston treat the problem of the prostitute
lightly, but in this play, he readily endorses the double standard
which, by permitting toleration of Freevill's actions while con-
demning Franceschina's, is, in effect, the cause of Franceschina's
difficulties. Early in the comedy when Malheureux fears for Freevill's excesses, Malheureux insists that he must bring him home
because he is concerned that the effects of wine, coupled with his
youth, will entice him to a brothel. Freevill comments on his
friend's uneasiness: "Most necessary buildings, Malheureux.
Ever since my intention of marriage, I do pray for their con-

tinuance. . . . I would have married men love the stews as English-
men lov'd the Low countries; wish war should be maintain'd
there lest it should come home to their own doors" (I.i. 59-60,
62-65). Freevill's endorsement of brothels seems to imply that
they keep a man's home sacrosanct. Without them, men might be
tempted to seek other men's wives to satisfy their sexual needs,
and thus make cuckolds of the lawful husbands. A further implication is that without the establishment of prostitution, an "honest" woman would not be safe.[30] Additionally, the wife is not
to be viewed as a sexual object. Sixteenth and seventeenth century theologians denounced lustful lovemaking even between
married couples.[31] Therefore, for gallants like Freevill, married
to a "lawful love," release could be found in the brothel; hence,
his contention that it was a necessity for the married man. During this same discourse on houses of prostitution, Freevill mentions: "Youth and appetite are above the club of Hercules" (I.i.
67). As earlier noted, a similar remark is made by Pompey to
Lord Escalus in *Measure for Measure* when the Duke intends to
close the brothels (see p. 48). It would seem that the Cavalier
playwrights accepted the brothel and the whore as a necessity of
life, for both Freevill and the gallant Cocledemoy offer en-
comiums on the instruction of prostitution.

Freevill's panegyric on the prostitute finds a counterpart in
The Honest Whore, Part II.[32] Freevill deems it a woman's occupation.[33] However, he does not fail to employ some satiric remarks indicating that the punk may repay you with the "French
crown." Freevill's coarser counterpart, Cocledemoy, a gallant
"of much money, some wit, but less honest" (I.i. 10-11), parallels his praise of bawds who sell the excellent virtues of virginity
and modesty, wholesale. And he concludes that they live in
"Clerkenwell" (a notorious haunt of rogues and whores) and
end their days in Bridewell.

Malheureux, the butt of the piece, denounces all whores.
As "one of professed abstinence" (I.ii. 109-110), with puritanical
proclivities, Malheureux, similar to Malvolio in *Twelfth Night,* is
foolish, and inflexible, and is to be viewed satirically. His moral
pretensions quickly shatter, and his brittle uprightness splinters
when both come in contact with hard reality.

While Malheureux suffers mildly, and the knave Cocledemoy bests Mulligrub, the puritanical vintner, it is Freevill, the

wit, in spite of his murky moral concerns, who reaps the rewards, and whose position most strongly identifies the Cavalier view. Freevill is the carefree, unconcerned gallant who finds no fault with his debonair behavior, who uses mistresses as a disposable throwaway, and who is fully confident that triumph is his due. An important ingredient required to leaven the mix which results in success for the wit is a young female innocent, preferably rich and well-born, who is always willing to love and submit totally to the gallant. Such fiction seems not too far removed from the reality, for women were in a weak position. Their options were seriously limited; marriage remained their only stronghold.

In *The Dutch Courtesan*, it is Beatrice, Freevill's betrothed, who vies for his favor and puts her trust in her future husband: "I give you faith; and, prithee,/Since, poor soul, I am so easy to believe thee,/Make it much more pity to deceive me" (II.i. 52-54). Beatrice, the gentle Elizabethan heroine—modest, manageable and artless—is fearful that these very virtuous qualities will jeopardize her love for him, and she makes a plea for mutual trust. Even though Franceschina declares she was Freevill's mistress, and Freevill (now supposedly dead) loved her ten thousand times more dearly than Beatrice, the self-effacing, ideal heroine cries: "O my heart! I will love you the better; I cannot hate what he affected" (IV.iv. 52-53). So undemanding, so unassuming is Beatrice that she never even expected her husband to be faithful. "Alas, I was not so ambitious of so supreme happiness that he should only love me; 'twas joy enough for me, poor soul, that I only might only love him" (IV.iv. 62-64).[34]

Believing Freevill dead, Beatrice laments her loss, and he is privy to her private thoughts. His "dove-like virgin without gall," is the embodiment of all the attributes so sought after in a wife and so often awarded to the Elizabethan gallants. Freevill eulogizes her most appealing qualities for him:

> With what a suff'ring sweetness, quiet modesty,
> Yet deep affection, she receiv'd my death!
> And then with what a patient, yet oppressed kindness
> She took my lewdly intimated wrongs!   (IV.v. 86-89)

Somehow, conscious of his own loose behavior and of his questionable morality, Freevill is particularly fearful of being fitted with horns. Consequently, he actually wants his wife to appear less attractive to other men; there is safety in such a solution. Freevill is a gallant whose moral center does not always hold, who can exploit those whom society dubs as unredeemable, and who can discover his own potential for contentment and security with a faithful wife in an ideal world. Freevill, the wit, like Lovewit in *The Alchemist,* and Winwife in *Bartholomew Fair,* breaks all the moral codes and is handed all of the rewards. He is cynical, witty, wilful and attractive, and the wages of his sin are a delight forever.

Totally different from her severely modest sister Beatrice, and scarcely a suitable spouse for one like Freevill, Crispinella is a creation that breathes freshness and a most modern viewpoint into an otherwise clear-cut Cavalier drama. She is indeed a character to be reckoned with, and many of her views, if taken seriously by the Beatrices of the Elizabethan Era, would have established inroads in areas that are only now being trod upon.

Similar to Lillia Bianca in *The Wild-Goose Chase* (Fletcher), but with a coarser tongue, Crispinella's contemporary views bear discussion. Her entrance is marked by a diatribe on the discomfiting custom of males familiarly kissing women.[35] Saucily, she pounces on those females who are hypocritical because they choose to be silent rather than to discuss certain taboo topics. She insists that honest and open speech is more natural: "She whose honest freeness makes it her virtue to speak what she thinks will make it her necessity to think what is good" (III.i. 37-39). She avows that that which is forbidden arouses the most desire: "As in the fashion of time, those books that are call'd in are most in sale and request, so in nature those actions that are most prohibited are most desired" (II.i. 41-44).

This independent woman even resents how fashion encumbers her movements and creates discomfort. Tysefew, who courts her, asks if she wears "high cork shoes—chopines?" and she replies: "Monstrous ones, I am, as many others are, piec'd above and piec'd beneath" (III.i. 106-108). Though she is short, she will not permit this to put her at a disadvantage or to make her feel inferior or ashamed: "What I made or can mend myself

I may blush at; but what nature put upon me, let her be ashamed for me, I ha'nothing to do with you. I forget my beauty" (III.i. 115-118).

Though Beatrice argues that "severe modesty is women's virtue" (III.i. 46-47), Crispinella chooses another definition for virtue: virtue is free and pleasant rather than harsh, austere and unkind.

Crispinella's views on marriage are most modern. She is convinced that as long as the man is still the suitor and subject to his lady, he is pleasant, pliable and deferential. But once he crosses the threshhold and becomes a husband, beware! The situation takes a 360 degree turn:

> When
> your husband is a suitor and under your choice,
> Lord, how supple he is, how obsequious, how
> at your service, sweet lady! Once married,
> got his head above, a stiff, crooked, knobby,
> inflexible, tyrannous creature he grows;
> then they turn like water, more you would em-
> brace, the less you hold.   (III.i. 73-78)

Given a choice, Crispinella's independence wins out: "I'll live my own woman, and if the worst come to the worst, I had rather prove a wag than a fool" (III.i. 79-80). When Beatrice argues how important a virtuous marriage is, Crispinella shows how often there is no kinship between the two: "Marriage, you know, is often without virtue, and virtue, I am sure, more oft without marriage" (III.i. 87-88). She also argues that women must accept all the disadvantages of marriage while men need not. Crispinella questions why women must marry. Men have a choice—"they may, and we must" (IV.i. 36).

When Freevill's father, Sir Lionel, attempts to propose marriage to her, Crispinella clearly defines the disadvantages, largely for the woman, in a "January-May" marriage. Judging from his father's aspirations, it might be fair to assume that Freevill, Jr. is descended from a line of gallants.

When Crispinella does agree to marry Tysefew subsequently,

he, too, has a few impressive requirements for his wife which betray his masculine superiority and negate the tenet of "matrimonial chastity":[36]

> My purse, my body, my heart is yours;
> only be silent in my house, modest at my table,
> and wanton in my bed. . . . (IV.i. 76-78)

Crispinella adds a dimension to *The Dutch Courtesan,* and her satire seems almost a feminine counterpart to *Epicoene;* she is, however, in essence, providing a serious critique of the double-standard marriage. The husband, ever the gallant, is free to continue his extra-marital activities and to follow his independent pursuits, while his wife must remain virtuous and submissive, and with "suff'ring sweetness" must bear his "contempt," "babble," or "unwholesome reversions," depending upon his particular deficiency. Crispinella's satirical comments categorize the inequities which her sister Beatrice will confront as Freevill's wife. While Crispinella bravely opts for independence, her aspirations fall short of the reality—she finally succumbs—she "must" marry, too.

In addition to raising the issues concomitant with the double-standard marriage, Marston, in his seriocomic vein, identifies the serious aspects of the prostitute's problem. Franceschina says, "Me ha' lost my will" (V.iii. 58), and is punished, Cavalier-fashion,—whipped and jailed.

Marston's evolution is toward the Cavalier vision—he rails neither against the reality of the prostitute's problem nor the brothel; his gallants triumph; his fools are gulled. Marston's sexual purveyors, like Jonson's and Shakespeare's, are laughed out of existence as he assures the audience that it is a "slight" play.

Whether possessed of wit, bearing, and brains, merely an ordinary drab, or occasionally a pernicious one, prostitutes are a constant on the Elizabethan scene, and the Cavalier dramatists are unanimous in their recognition of this verity. Whores are allowed to survive—to ply their trade and to entertain—but the whores in the Cavalier comedies are never offered the opportunity to succeed in escaping their destiny.

NOTES

[1] See Alfred Harbage, *Shakespeare and the Rival Traditions* (New York: The Macmillan Company, 1952), p. 161, who is in agreement with this position. Gabriel Jackson, *Vision and Judgment in Ben Jonson's Drama* (New Haven: Yale University Press, 1968), p. 165, maintains that Jonson's position is basically idealistic, though his unrepentant conspiratorial characters are accepted back into a tainted society which they reflect. Edward B. Partridge, *The Broken Compass* (New York: Columbia University Press, 1958), p. 69, judges Jonson as a strict moralist.

[2] See Judd Arnold, *A Grace Peculiar: Ben Jonson's Cavalier Heroes,* The Pennsylvania State University Studies, 36 (University Park: Pennsylvania State University, 1972), p. 7, for this interpretation. While Arnold agrees that Jonson's view of the gallant as triumphant wit is antithetical to that of the reformer, with whom Jonson cannot be categorized, Arnold maintains it is because Jonson "has so clearly defined the impossibility of his [the reformer's] task." My view is that it is less the formidable task (so readily acceptable to the dramatist who is the exponent of the Puritan view) which deters Jonson, and rather the more pragmatic acceptance of the real world, which belief, albeit, carries with it overtones of cynicism.

[3] Plot: Leaving the city because of plague, Master Lovewit puts his house in the care of his butler Jeremy, known to his underworld friends as Face. He invites swindler Subtle, posing as an alchemist, and prostitute Dol Common, to join him in using the house for their knavish business. The three are successful in their cozenage until Face and Subtle argue over authority. Sensitive to the fact that such a disruption will ruin their successful operation, Dol manages to effect a peaceful settlement. In their moneymaking schemes all three exploit a parade of gulls who are either naive, ambitious or greedy.

[4] Ben Jonson, *The Alchemist,* ed. Alvin B. Kernan (New Haven: Yale University Press, 1974). All further references are to this edition.

[5] See Partridge, pp. 124-125. "Face is playing on the grammatical

and logical senses in Dol's last name, then moving on to other terms suggested by 'Common.' A common noun is applicable to each of the individuals which makes up a class or genus. It belongs to more than one, as Dol does. More generally, common means public or free to be used by everyone. 'Proper' and 'Singular' also have both grammatical and more general meanings which contrast wittily, each making the common Dol something more special than she is. . . . The height of this is 'Particular,' which means 'private person, not public' (OED). Partridge notes further, "Drawing lots seems to be their [Face and Sublte's] way of determining the fate of women. . .", see p. 143.

[6]The main plot of *Bartholomew Fair* deals with Justice Adam Overdo, who, in disguise, mingles with the people at the Fair to seek out criminals and to record lawlessness. Suspecting Ursula, a seller of roast pig and beer, Overdo stops at her booth to test her. As he drinks, various underworld characters enter the booth.

Another aspect of the story deals with Winwife, a London gallant, who came courting Dame Purecraft, a widow who lived with her daughter, Win-the-Fight, and her son-in-law, John Littlewit. Littlewit disclosed to Winwife that Dame Purecraft had been told by fortune-tellers that she would marry a madman within a week; therefore, Littlewit suggested to him that he imitate his companion, Tom Quarlous, who pretends madness.

Also at the Fair is Grace Wellborn, the ward of Justice Overdo, whom he is pressuring to marry young Bartholomew Cokes, a rich, doltish country gentleman, and brother to Overdo's wife. In another part of the Fair, Winwife and Quarlous, who had attracted Grace away from her group, drew swords to decide a dispute as to who should have Cokes' attractive young fiancee. Grace prevailed upon them not to fight and devised another plan. She suggested that each man write a word on a table, and the first passerby was to choose the word he preferred. The winner of her hand would thus be determined, since Grace had quite decided that Cokes would not suit her as a husband.

A sub-plot deals with three knaves: Capt. Whit, a bawd; Knockum, a horse trader; and Edgeworth, a cutpurse, who enlist Mrs. Littlewit and Mrs. Overdo as temporary prostitutes at the Fair.

[7]The main plot of *Epicoene* deals with Dauphine's attempts as legitimate heir, to get his Uncle Morose's money settled on him. The name Morose is indicative of the man and is in sharp contrast to his scheming high-spirited nephew. Though Dauphine's friends have some familiarity with his campaign against his uncle, they are not privy to all his plans. There are also two sub-plots. The first centers on a group of blue-stockings, the Collegiate Women. They are initially characterized as affected and egotistical and then shown as dissolute. Their actions have no direct importance on Dauphine's machinations. The second sub-plot deals with the gulling of Sir Amorous La Foole and Sir John Daw, but similar to the Collegiate Women, they are only

a contributory factor to Dauphine's ends. Truewit is Dauphine's ally and master of the revels in both sub-plots; however, he has no major part in the primary action of the play; namely, the attempt to secure the legacy. All three plots reach a denouement concurrently.

[8] Ben Jonson, *Epicoene,* ed. Edward Partridge (New Haven: Yale University Press, 1971). All further references are to this edition.

[9] Harbage, p. 190.

[10] *Ibid.,* p. 192.

[11] *Ibid.*

[12] A. C. Bradley, *Shakespearean Tragedy* (New York: World Publishing Company, 1962), p. 36.

[13] Bradley, p. 40.

[14] Plot: After the battle of Shrewsbury many false reports were circulated among the peasants. The truth of valiant Hotspur's death at the hands of Prince Henry, and King Henry's pledge to crush the rebellion by squashing the opposition, confirmed that the rebel forces had not been successful.

Meanwhile, Falstaff dallied in carrying out his orders to proceed north and recruit troops for the King. Involved with Mistress Quickly, he exploited his royal commission to avoid imprisonment for debt. With Prince Henry, who had ignored the war, he continued his rioting and jesting until both were called to march with the army against the rebels.

As King Henry lay dying, not even John's victory could cheer up the old king. Asking God's forgiveness, the King counseled Prince Henry to commit his powerful lords to foreign wars in order to alleviate domestic difficulties.

The prince, now King Henry V, reprimanded Falstaff for his behavior and told him that until he mended his ways, he was banished, on pain of death, to a distance of ten miles away from Henry's person. Seemingly undaunted, Falstaff explains to his boon companions that he yet would make them important, that the King would send for him, and they would carry on in their old, carefree ways.

Prince John, pleased with Henry's new public image, prophesies that England would be at war with France before the year was out.

[15] Plot: Concerned with the political and moral corruption of Vienna, the locale of the play, Duke Vicentio appoints Angelo, a respected and intelligent city official, as deputy governor to enforce existing laws. The Duke then pretends to leave for Poland but actually disguises himself as a frair to watch the outcome of Angelo's reforms.

Angelo's first act is to imprison Claudio, a young nobleman who has gotten his betrothed, Juliet, with child. Under an old statute, now revived by Angelo, Claudio's offense is punishable by death. Through Lucio, a rakish friend, Claudio asks his sister Isabella, a young novice about to take her vows as a nun, to intercede for him with the new governor. Meeting with little success at first, Isabella then learns that she may obtain her brother's release if she will yield to Angelo's lustful desires. Though Claudio is originally revolted by this idea, he finally begs his sister to give herself to Angelo. Horrified, Isabella lashes out at Claudio for his cowardice. Having overheard much of the conversation, the Friar/Duke suggests a plan to save Claudio to Isabella. He then tells her that Angelo had been betrothed to Mariana, a high-born lady, but because of a problem with her dowry, Angelo consequently broke the vows, hinting at dishonor in Mariana. The plan is for Isabella to rendezvous with Angelo; then Mariana is to be substituted.

All goes as arranged, but Angelo, fearing public exposure, breaks his promise to release Claudio. The Friar/Duke intervenes again, and instead of executing Claudio, has him hidden, and sends Angelo the head of another prisoner who had died of natural causes. The Duke allows Isabella to believe that Claudio is dead. Isabella and Mariana denounce Angelo as a traitor and virgin-violator. At the end, Angelo is saved from death by the pleas of both women. Mariana marries Angelo; Isabella marries the Duke.

[16]See William W. Lawrence, *Shakespeare's Problem Comedies,* 2nd ed. (New York: F. Ungar Publishing Company, 1960), p. 50, who asserts that the term "problem play" applies "to all those productions which clearly do not fall into the category of tragedy, and yet are too serious and analytic to fit the commonly accepted conception of comedy." For further discussions on Shakespeare's problem plays, see: E. M. W. Tillyard, *Shakespeare's Problem Comedies* (London, 1950); A. Quiller-Couch and J. Dover Wilson, editors of the New Cambridge edition of *Measure for Measure* (Cambridge University Press, 1922); Arthur Sewell, *Character and Society in Shakespeare* (Oxford, 1951); and *Shakespeare's Problem Comedies,* edited by Robert Ornstein (D. C. Heath, 1961).

[17]See Chilton Latham Powell, *English Domestic Relations 1487-1653* (New York: Russell and Russell, 1972), pp. 37-40, for a discussion of the legality of spousals *de praesenti.* Powell asserts: "The church, from the beginning of the Christian era on, had attempted to put the emphasis upon solemnization, although it always recognized a privately contracted marriage as valid. Luther's teachings, on the other hand, while retaining the church service as a beneficial custom, threw the emphasis upon the previous contract, where in the light of actual law it belonged. . . . Thus, in England as well as elsewhere, marriage by means of spousals *de praesenti* was recognized by both church and state, but the church had managed to become accredited as the proper authority for the solemnization of it. Nevertheless, as this authority was self-assumed and as the sacramental character of marriage was repudiated in the *Thirty-Nine Articles of 1552,* it had only the validity of tradition."

[18]Though Juliet is held to be more responsible for the "offenceful" act, it is Claudio who is paying for this act with his life. However, because Juliet is pregnant, she escapes the same fate.

[19]Plot: Prince Pericles of Tyre went to Antioch to seek the hand of the beautiful princess whose father had developed an unnatural passion for her, and who slew suitors that could not answer the riddle the King posed. Pericles solved the riddle which disclosed an incestuous relationship between the King and his daughter, but he prudently feared to reveal his knowledge. Convinced that his life was in danger, Pericles fled and outwitted the agents sent by Antiochus to kill him.

Back in Tyre, Pericles feared that Antiochus would ravage his city and decided to save Tyre by taking a journey until Antiochus died. With his crew, he landed on the remote Greek province of Tarsus and was made welcome by the rulers, Cleon and his wife Dionyza. Still pursued by Antiochus's agents, Pericles left Tarsus, was shipwrecked, and as the only survivor landed in King Simonides' court in Pentapolis. The King's daughter, Thaisa, fell in love with Pericles, and they were married.

In the meantime, Antiochus and his daughter died, and Pericles was importuned to return to take the crown of Tyre. Thaisa, due to give birth, took the voyage to Tyre, but the ship was overtaken by storm. Seemingly dead after giving birth to a daughter, Thaisa was placed in a watertight casket and drifted ashore to Epheseus. Pericles, having reached Tarsus safely, left the child Marina with Cleon and Dionyza, and set sail for Tyre.

Thaisa, revived by a skilled physician, but believing her husband and child lost at sea, took the veil of a votaress to the goddess Diana. Pericles continued to rule alone in Tyre. Marina, superior to the daughter of Cleon and Dionyza, incurred their jealousy, and they planned to have her killed. Without their knowledge, the plan was aborted; instead, pirates captured Marina and sold her to a brothel owner in Mytilene.

In Tarsus, meanwhile, Dionyza persuaded Cleon to erect a monument to Marina's memory as a safety precaution against Pericles' rage. Pericles' grief at seeing the monument when he came to reclaim his daughter made him sink into endless mourning and leave Tarsus.

In Mytilene, Marina confounded the brothel owners by remaining a virgin and earning her living by virtuous arts; she also won the heart of Gov. Lysimachus. Pericles, now a distracted wanderer, came to Mytilene. He then discovered Marina was his daughter and was reunited with his wife, Thaisa, through the goddess Diana. Pericles and Thaisa reigned in Pentapolis; Lysimachus and Mariana, as man and wife, ruled over Tyre.

[20]Since virginity was so highly prized, deflowering the novitiate was very profitable for the brothelkeeper. Consequently, deluding the client by falsely offering the seasoned prostitute as a pure maiden (achieved with tricks of the trade), was a common practice. See also p. 87, when Frank Gullman's mother, also her bawd in *A Mad World, My Masters,* boasts that

she has already sold her daughter's maidenhead fifteen times and plans to continue.

[21]Women betray women in Middleton's plays, *Women Beware Women* and *A Mad World, My Masters;* also Cyril Tourneur's *The Revenger's Tragedy.*

[22]Plot: The King of France lay ill of a disease that might be cured by only one physician who was now dead, but who had bequeathed to his daughter, Helena, all his books and papers on cures for disease.

Bertram, the Count of Rousillon, served the king, and Helena was the ward of his mother, the Countess of Rousillon, who loved her as a daughter. Helena loved Bertram, but he saw her as a social inferior. Through her knowledge of the King's illness, Helena devised a plan to make Bertram her husband. Offering her life as a forfeit if she failed to cure the King, she would, however, ask for the lord of her choice in marriage, if she succeeded. Cured, the King ordered the marriage to Bertram to be performed at once. Bending to the King's will, Bertram consented only to a legal marriage but deserted Helena after the ceremony, informing his mother that he would never accept a forced marriage. He specifically told Helena that she would not really be his wife until she wore on her finger a ring he now wore on his, and carried in her body a child that was his. But these two things would never come to pass since Bertram vowed never to see her again.

Disguising herself as a religious pilgrim, Helena followed Bertram to Italy, where he had gone to fight for the Duke of Florence. Lodging with a widow and her beautiful and virtuous daughter Diana, Helena learned that Bertram had seduced a number of young Florentine girls and was now pressing his attentions on Diana. Confiding in them that she was Bertram's wife, Diana agreed to Helena's plot against Bertram. Diana had an assignation with Bertram, and Helena was substituted, and got Bertram's ring.

News came to the Countess in France and to Bertram in Italy that Helena had died of grief and love for Bertram. Bertram, restored to the King's favor, and about to be betrothed to the lovely and wealthy daughter of a favorite lord, when the King noticed the ring Bertram was wearing, recognizing it as the jewel he had given Helena. Bertram insisted it was the jewel of a high-born lady who had loved him but had not been free to wed him.

At that moment Diana appeared as a petitioner to the King and demanded that Bertram fulfill his pledge to recognize her as his wife. After the confusion is cleared up, Helena appears, explains the situation, and declares that she has fulfilled the requirements for becoming Bertram's wife: she had his ring on her finger and was carrying his child.

[23]Plot: In the main plot, Freevill and Malheureux are friends with conflicting views. Freevill is a rakish young man and Malheureux is one who professes abstinence. When Freevill decides to marry, he turns over his mistress Franceschina to his friend, and in spite of all his good intentions, Mal-

heureux falls totally in love with the prostitute. Franceschina becomes vicious when Freevill tosses her away, and she plans to have him murdered, but her plot is uncovered and she is punished.

One sub-plot deals with Cocledemoy, a rich rogue who freely indulges himself in whatever pleasures him. He takes special joy in gulling the puritan Mulligrum

Crispinella, the sister of Freevill's "lawful love," Beatrice, is being courted by Tysefew. She is clever, crisp and her constant banter with Tysefew airs many of the more emancipated views regarding the male/female role and the marriage relationship in the seventeenth century.

[24]T. S. Eliot, *Selected Essays* (New York: Harcourt Brace, 1950), p. 110.

[25]See Arnold Davenport, ed. *Poems of John Marston* (Liverpool: Liverpool University Press, 1961), p. 11, who finds Marston a disillusioned cynic and a Calvinist. Philip J. Finkelpearl, *John Marston of the Middle Temple* (Cambridge: Harvard University Press, 1969), p. 258, and Oscar J. Campbell, *Comicall Satyre and Shakespeare's "Troilus and Cressida"* (San Marino: Huntington Library Publications, 1938), p. 184, corroborate the view of Marston as moralist. Una Ellis-Fermor, *The Jacobean Drama*, 4th ed. rev. (London: Methuen & Co., Ltd., 1961), p. 78, finds his comedy "representative of the age" with "implications of social satire." C. S. Lewis, *English Literature in the Sixteenth Century* (Oxford, England: Clarendon Press, 1954), p. 474, and Alfred Harbage, *Shakespeare and the Rival Traditions* (New York: The Macmillan Company, 1952), p. 78, are skeptical of Marston's sincerity and morality and find his plays tasteless and gross. Between these extremes, Thomas M. Parrott and Robert H. Ball, *A Short View of Elizabethan Drama* (New York: Charles Scribner's Sons, 1958), p. 153, identify him as an innovator of "realistic-satiric comedy" which is "amoral rather than ethical." See M. L. Wine, ed. of *The Dutch Courtesan* by John Marston, Regents Renaissance Series (Lincoln: University of Nebraska Press, 1965), p. xxiii, whose view tends to reinforce the Cavalier vision—a light-hearted, cynical treatment. Wine finds that Marston "minimizes the seriousness of the theme and invites the audience to laugh at the play with him." Wine further asserts that Marston has no interest in *The Dutch Courtesan* in dealing with "problems of prostitution," nor "with the plight of the whore who wants to reform but is prevented by the very men who condemn her trade."

[26]John Marston, *The Dutch Courtesan*, ed. M. L. Wine (Lincoln: University of Nebraska Press, 1965). All further references are to this edition.

[27]See Burford, p. 78. He mentions that there were many Dutch whorehouses on the Bankside which were well-run and much frequented. He believes that these immigrants brought much expertise and new concepts, possibly even improved health and hygiene standards. However, Burford maintains that the Flemish bawds were often the recipients of abuse and attack. See also pp. 145-146. By the turn of the century (about 1600), the Manor House became known as "Hollands Laager," and later became the most famous brothel of its day under the name of "Holland's Leaguer."

[28]See footnotes, pp. 18-19 in *Dutch Courtesan*. "Cockatrice"—a term used for prostitute. "Suppository"—Freevill's designation of suppository is that which would be administered by a tube or a pipe for a whore and has a sexual connotation.

[29]See footnote, p. 28, in *Dutch Courtesan*. "Serpigo"—a general term for creeping or spreading skin diseases (OED), but associated here with venereal disease.

[30]Back in Roman times, Cato the Censor (234-149 B.C.), a man much concerned with virtue, was of the same opinion and endorsed prostitution: "Blessed be they as virtuous who when they feel their virile members swollen with lust, visit a brothel rather than grind at some husband's private mill." Tacitus, *Annals,* Book II, 85. See also Henriques, p. 24, who notes St. Augustine's views on prostitution: "Suppress prostitution, and capricious lusts will otherthrow society."

[31]See Lawrence Stone, *The Family, Sex and Marriage in England 1500-1800* (New York: Harper & Row, 1977), p. 499. He states: "In England, the consensus of theological opinion also stressed the prime importance of 'matrimonial chastity,' as it was called . . . " which, Stone notes, "was not in conflict with the Protestant view of 'holy matrimony' as a source of mutual comfort as well as a means of satisfying lust and procreating legitimate children. . . ." Stone adds: "By 'matrimonial chastity' was meant moderation of sexual passion. . . . All passionate love-making was sinful, regardless of whether it took place inside or outside marriage." See also Camden, p. 118, who notes that manners and talk between husband and wife must be totally pure and moral. Vives quotes Eusebius saying that the husband has to refrain from "unclean sportes," as well as plays and "filthye touchinges," or he may give the appearance of being a lover rather than a husband.

[32]Hippolito reverses his stand on harlotry based on his unabated passion for Bellafront, and he debates the benefits of being a whore. His main argument is that the whore is completely free; men are her slaves; she is much sought after by gentlemen and soldiers (IV.i. 329-359).

[33]See Vern L. Bullough, *The Subordinate Sex* (Baltimore: Penguin Books, Inc., paperback 1974), p. 24. He notes that law codes such as the Hammurabic Code permit women only three occupations: tavernkeepers, priestesses and prostitutes.

[34]While Beatrice is the perfect, virtuous heroine, it would seem that these qualities of modesty and selflessness would eventually pall on such a gallant as Freevill, and he would seek out the brothel or other similar activity to overcome the boredom of his home. An example of such an excess of piety and goodness, which results in tragedy, is Isabella, wife of Brachiano in *The White Devil* (Webster).

[35]See Stone, p. 520. "Another indication of English attitudes . . . was the custom in England for persons of different sexes to greet each other by a kiss upon the lips. . . . A young woman in one of Marston's plays complained "tis grown one of the most unsavory ceremonies . . . any fellow . . . must salute us on the lips'." For a very different view, written when Erasmus was a young man, see *The Correspondence of Erasmus, Letters 1-141, 1484-1500*, trans. R. A. B. Mynors and D. F. S. Thompson, Annotated by Wallace K. Ferguson, Vol. I (Toronto and Buffalo: University of Toronto Press, 1974), pp. 192-193. Letter #103 England [Summer] 1499, written to Fausto Andrelini. ". . . there is, besides, one custom which can never be commended too highly. When you arrive anywhere, you are received with kisses on all sides, and when you take your leave they speed you on your way with kisses. The kisses are renewed when you come back. When guests come to your house, their arrival is pledged with kisses; and when they leave, kisses are shared once again. If you should happen to meet, then kisses are given profusely. In a word, wherever you turn, the world is full of kisses. If you too, Fausto, once tasted the softness and fragrance of these same kisses, I swear you would yearn to live abroad in England; and not for ten years only, in the manner of Solon, but all your lifelong period."

[36]See note 31, p. 73.

CHAPTER II

THE LIBERAL VIEW

The Liberal attitude toward the whore, though more compassionate than that of the Cavalier, continues to respond to a realistic universe, one where the wit still wins out, where imperfect moral justice reigns, but one which seeks to approach the problem of the prostitute with a less jaundiced view. Beatings and Bridewell are eschewed. If the whore hopes to escape her destiny, she is permitted one option—marriage—but not to the wit or to the original seducer; instead, she is offered the consolation prize, the man who cannot object to her sullied state. Unlike the Cavalier portrayal, the Liberal playwright tends to treat the harlot with less disdain and with more sympathy. She is often a more individualized character who has intelligence and ability and who feels that marriage, even to a dubious male, is preferable to her present state. Adaptable and aware that the maladroit squandering of her reputation leaves her with few choices, she is most willing to renounce her present profession in favor of marriage, the only avenue of escape from the desperation of her destiny.

There are many examples of comedies which resolve the prostitute's problem by "fubbing" her off in marriage, such as Frances in *Ram Alley* (Barry); Doll in *Northward Ho* (Dekker and Webster); Sindefy in *Eastward Ho* (Chapman, Jonson and Marston); Julia and Francessina in *The Woman Hater* (Beaumont); Phoebe in *A Mad Couple Well Matched* (Brome); Phryne in *The Jealous Lovers* (Randolph); Clariflora in *The Knave in Grain New Vamped* ("J. D."); Mrs. Wagtail in *A Woman Is a Weathercock* (Field); and Florida and Felecia in *The Fleire* (Sharpham). Middleton's Liberal portrayal of this type of courtesan—one who welcomes marriage as the only viable release from a fate which relegates her to society's underbelly— is the best and fullest treatment of this category and, therefore, the most rewarding; consequently, this chapter will focus on Middleton's depiction as represented in *A Trick to Catch the Old One*, *A Mad World, My Masters*, and *Michaelmas Term*.

THOMAS MIDDLETON

Critics disagree as to Middleton's point of view; he has been categorized not only as a realist, a romanticist, a didactic moralist, a satirist, and an interpreter of the contemporary economic struggle, but his outlook has also been classified as impersonal, amoral, and even immoral.[1]

As a dramatist, Middleton's vision is that the world, unfortunately, is not Utopian, and he perceives it as imperfect. Revealing a cynical vein, he reminds us that to see society from the pious view of virtue is to stitch together the Emperor's new clothes with the thread of unreality and naiveté. Bending to a harsh environment and compromising is, lamentably, "the way of the world," for it is difficult to remain unsullied in a society that renders imperfect moral justice. Middleton exhorts us to live within our limitations. He finds foolishness unforgivable in comedy, and wit for the comic hero remains more important than morality.

As a commodity in the marriage market, the whore is tainted merchandise, and the discovery of even one night's frolic wrecks forever a woman's chance of an honorable marriage in Renaissance drama. Such a premise, already noted, while totally true in Cavalier comedies, begins to erode as the Liberal playwrights attempt to marry off the whore and to give her a respected status in society.[2] While marriage may now help the whore escape her destiny, the moral defective still remains a handicapped player in the marriage game, a game taxing even to the most capable contestants.

A Trick To Catch The Old One[3]

Middleton's stance assumes that one must, with good grace, adapt to the pitfalls and the faults of a faulty universe.[4]   The finest example of his treatment of the subject occurs in *A Trick To Catch The Old One*. The slipshod justice arises when Jane, who should rightfully have been rewarded with the wit, Witgood, must content herself, as a cast-off mistress, with the consolation prize of an aged suitor. She makes the best of an unfair situation; she accepts Old Hoard, society's "hand-me-down," with good grace. Such a resolution reflects Middleton's Liberal approach regarding the plight of the prostitute. It addresses itself to compromise in an imperfect society—palming off the prostitute in marriage in preference to Bridewell—as the most rational and humane response in an often irrational cosmos.

Witgood's opening comment, "All's gone! still thou'rt a gentleman, that's all; but a poor one, that's nothing" (I.i. 1-2), immediately identifies him as the gallant who has the confidence in his background and breeding which assures him that poverty will not serve as an obstacle with such aristocratic advantages. In that same speech he wonders: "Well, how should a man live now that has no living, hum?" (I.i. 22-23). And his immediate reply to this question assures us that wit is his weapon: "Why, are there not a million of men in the world that only sojourn upon their brain, and make their wits their mercers; and am I but one amongst that million, and cannot thrive upon 't?" (I.i. 23-27). And he is quite ready to embark upon any adventure, "any trick, out of the compass of law" (I.i. 27-28).

Since Witgood has lost his possessions through his own folly as a wastethrift, he can only hope to win the rich Joyce with Jane's help. But, irked by his present plight, he blames his courtesan for his ruin and berates her for that fraility for which she is already suffering. The rake first violates the woman and then cites her debauched status as proof of her immorality. Such sophistry is the hook on which the profligate hangs his deception. When the courtesan greets him with "My love!" he replies: "My loathing! hast thou been the secret consumption of my purse, and now com'st to undo my last means, my wits? Wilt leave no virtue in me, and yet thou ne'er the better?/Hence, courtesan, round-webb'd tarantula,/That dryest the roses in the cheeks of youth!" (I.i. 29-35). Wounded by his venomous remarks, she admonishes him:

> I've been true unto your pleasure; and all your lands
> Thrice rack'd was never worth the jewel which
> I prodigally gave you, my virginity.
> Lands mortgag'd may return, and more esteem'd;
> But honesty once pawn'd is ne'er redeem'd.   (I.i. 36-40)

Aware that his outburst is bitter and unreasonable, Witgood recants: "Forgive; I do thee wrong/To make thee sin, and then to chide thee for 't" (I.i. 41-42).

While Middleton's witty hero starts out as an egotistical uncaring gallant, much in accord with the Cavalier view, he tends to become more sympathetic to the whore, or more Puritan in his approach. Witgood recants. Middleton's sub-plot with Dampit and Audrey sharply reflects the disdain in which the prostitute is held and tends to support the Cavalier view.[5]

Witgood's attitude softens toward Jane, but she is still sufficiently pragmatic to realize that he is ready to cast her off. She is his "loathing" now; nevertheless, Witgood still expects that his cast-off mistress will give him her total loyalty and support: "Dost love me?   Fate has so cast it that all my means/I must derive from thee" (I.i. 50-52). Jane willingly promises to carry out his scheme, and Witgood's reply is: "Spoke like/An honest drab, i'faith" (I.i. 65-66). Though Witgood is her original seducer and only sexual partner, he continues to refer to her as "courtesan," and even in this instance, though he is dependent upon her, he flippantly refers to her as a "drab." While Jane's cooperation bespeaks a loyalty to the undeserving Wit, the Courtesan is well aware of how hopeless her present situation is: "I begin to applaud thee; our states being desperate, they are soon resolute" (I.i. 67-68).   Though Jane has uncomplainingly accepted the universally applied double standard—the hero's rejection of the fallen woman—she still hopes to patch up her existence with a marriage which will lend respectability to her state. Though she may originally have cherished the idea of marriage to her lover Witgood, this notion is quickly dispelled at the outset of the play.

Content to fall in with Witgood's intrigues, Jane plays her part of the rich widow with a strong sense of authenticity and credibility which insures Witgood's success in gaining his ends.

It is she who outlines how perfectly she will manage the part of his wealthy widow: "Arm your wits then/Speedily; there shall want nothing in me./Either in behavior, discourse, or fashion,/ That shall discredit your intended purpose./I will so artfully disguise my wants,/And set so good a courage on my state./That I shall be believed" (I.i. 76-82). Though Jane may be a country girl whom Witgood has sullied, the perfection of her performance demonstrates not only her goodwill, but her familiarity with conduct, conversation and fashion, and supports the rationale that Jane's knowledge may have been more than merely superficial. Either these arts were inherent in her background, or her close contact with landed gentry sharpened her keen perception and permitted her to develop them. The validity with which Jane enacts her role as a rich lady adds weight to the assumption that she may have come from an upperclass family and was a woman of ability and acuity who had blundered into the realm of sin.

Throughout the play Witgood exploits all to gain his goals—the Host, Lucre and Hoard, and particularly the Courtesan. Because of her imperfect situation and tarnished reputation, Jane chooses to comply with his sometimes less-than-moral schemes.

In Jane's dealings with Hoard and Lucre for Witgood's benefit, she is keenly aware of their weaknesses, and by her deft psychological appraisal, she is able to assess the precise moment to assault their vulnerability. Jane does not overtly deceive Hoard. Hers is an act of omission rather than commission. She is honest, but also sufficiently sophisticated to allow for Hoard's greed, so that it operates on her behalf.

The gusty animal spirits of both old men are undeniably attractive and the basis of their rivalry would seem to be a need to provoke each other, as Hoard outlines early in the drama: "Pecunius Lucre, if ever fortune so bless me that I may be at leisure to vex thee, or any means so favor me that I may have opportunity to mad thee, I will pursue it with that flame of hate, that spirit of malice, unrepressed wrath, that I will blast thy comforts" (I.iii. 40-45). When courting the courtesan, whom he mistakenly believes to be wealthy, Hoard feels that "in this one chance" of winning her "shines a twice-happy fate;/I both deject my foe and raise my state" (II.ii. 79-80). Once he is launched on this venture, his vigor, high spirits and business man's mentality create a situation which permits Jane to play on his naiveté and deceive him by being totally truthful. When she says, "Alas, you love not widows but for wealth!/I promise you I ha' nothing, sir" (III.i. 220-221), Hoard responds to her apparently ingenuous duplicity: "Well said, widow,/Well said; thy love is all I seek. . ."(III.i. 222-223). Renouncing Hoard's fictitious rival Witgood, she says: "On my knees I vow/He ne'er shall marry me" (III.i. 201-202). Witgood, peeping in, replies: "Heaven knows he never meant it!" (III.i. 203). All of the irony is richly humorous and Jane's supposedly artless behavior and forceful performance culminate in Hoard's self-congratulatory exclamation: "Not only in joy, but I in wealth excel:/No more sweet widow, but, sweet wife, farewell" (III.i. 249-250).

In spite of his cozenage, the Courtesan manages every crisis once they are married, and it is she who copes with the problems that plague Hoard. When he is hemmed in by his adversary and fears to let him enter, it is Jane who decides: "Let him in peaceably; . . . You may stand by and smile at his old weakness:/Let me alone to answer him" (IV.i. 20-24). Learning that he has been outwitted, Lucre rebukes her. Her poignant reply, while still impersonating the widow, rather sharply reveals the sentiments of the role-playing widow as well as the disillusioned love of Witgood's mistress:

> I do confess
> I lov'd your nephew; nay, I did affect him
> Against the mind and liking of my friends;
> Believ'd his promises; lay here in hope
> Of flatter'd living, and the boast of lands.
> Coming to touch his wealth and state indeed,
> It appears dross; I find him not the man;
> Imperfect, mean, scarce furnish'd of his needs;
> In words, fair lordships; in performance, hovels.
> Can any woman love the thing that is not?   (IV.i. 50-58)

Surely, Witgood seduced her with promises, promises which later turned out to be nothing more than mere words. But, because she is such an unusual woman—venturesome, vital, and unselfish —she does not permit her disenchantment (unlike the Dutch Courtesan) to make her bitter and ungenerous. She knows that as a courtesan—even a reformed one—her options are limited. She knows also that Witgood's promises were never meant to be kept: "If words were lands, your nephew would be rich" (IV.i. 74). Illusion and self-deception are now totally alien to Jane, for surely, how else could such a pretty and intelligent woman bring herself to marry an old man in place of her handsome young lover: "Do you think i'faith,/That I could twine such a dry oak as this,/Had promise in your nephew took effect?" (I.i. 67-69).

Because Jane recognizes her desperate state, she is most anxious to marry Old Walkadine Hoard, to reform, and to gain respectability: "I'm yet like those whose riches lie in dreams;/ If I be wak'd, they're false, such is my fate,/Who venture deeper than the desperate state./Though I have sinn'd, yet could I become new,/For where I once vow, I am ever true" (IV.iv. 146-150).

Though Jane suffers for her transgressions, Witgood achieves his ends. Witgood's methods are not very scrupulous, and Jane begins to resent his use of her to further his plans. The Courtesan, pressing Hoard to pay Witgood's creditors, remarks to Witgood: "But methinks, i'faith, you might have made some shift to discharge this yourself, having in the mortgage, and never have burd'ned my conscience with it" (IV.iv. 182-185).

As for conscience, this is not Witgood's strong point. Were he truly moral and not merely a self-seeking gallant, he would have married his courtesan. However, as a "gentleman," and adhering to a code which encourages young men of the upper classes to use women outside of their class for pre-marital sex experiences, Witgood feels free to prevail upon and profit from his courtesan, Jane. Perhaps, the conscience Witgood exhibits is in his desire to see Jane safely married to rich Old Hoard: "Whence, make up thy own fortunes now; do thyself a good turn once in thy days: He's rich . . . he's an old doating fool, . . . marry him . . . 't would ease my conscience well to see thee well bestowed; I have a care of thee, i'faith" (III.i. 115-121).

Aside from this tiny prick of conscience, Witgood never feels or is held responsible for his behavior. Jane had hoped to marry Witgood, but when her situation became desperate, she was most willing to marry Old Hoard. Witgood, however, is so lacking in integrity that he suggests to Jane that she play the role of the rake and feel free to cuckold Hoard because he is an old man. Witgood broaches this course of action when the Courtesan reveals that Hoard wishes to marry her: ". . . you've fell upon wealth enough, and there's young gentlemen enow can help you to the rest" (III.i. 254-256).

Though there continues to be a good deal of discussion concerning conscience throughout the play, little of it seems to govern most of the players. For example, Lucre promises to return the mortgage to Witgood to insure his marriage to the rich widow since Lucre, too, may profit.

While I am in agreement with Middleton's essential vision— one must survive and make the best of an imperfect world—it seems to me that Witgood's celebration of life hurts others, for in a born-to-the-purple manner, he exploits all who can benefit him. Even his fiancee Joyce is made to suffer because he elects to have an illicit affair with the Courtesan, and in trying to rid himself of his debts, he inflicts further suffering upon her while he is ostensibly wooing the rich widow. Joyce reveals her hurt: "Why dost thou flatter thy affections so,/With name of him that for a widow's bed/Neglects thy purer love?" (III.ii. 10-12).

While the rake is occasionally punished in Jacobean drama, one would be hard-pressed to support this assertion from the conclusion of this comedy, as well as from others I have cited. Generally, the witty hero wins the maiden, while the more "frail" female, if fortunate, gets the less-than-manly male. Cool, clever and conscienceless, the last act finds Witgood winning the "good" girl and the gold.[6]

As Witgood celebrates his triumph in the last act, Hoard discovers that he has been tricked into marrying a whore. Hoard recoils: "Out, out! I am cheated; infinitely cozen'd!" (V.ii 106). But Jane points out to him that his greed was the cause of his folly: "If in disgrace you share,/I sought not you;/You pursued me, nay forc'd me. . ." (V.ii. 136-137). She reminds him that she did not deceive him nor was she dishonest. Frankly assessing her fallen state as not the most "odious" and that "worse has been forgiven" (V.ii. 145), assuming rightfully that

Old Hoard admits that "she's young, she's fair, she's wise" (IV.iv. 6-7), and granting that marriage to a fallen woman "save[s] a sinner" and frees the husband "from a cuckold for ever" (V.ii. 151-152), the Courtesan thus consoles her husband.

In the final disavowal of her former harlotry, the Courtesan catalogs a medley of tricks which married women make use of in order to attract lovers, to keep assignations, and to cuckold their husbands, tricks similar to those employed by the Collegiate women in *Epicoene.*

At the end, the Courtesan is happy with Hoard, and he has the good sense and good humor to realize his own folly and to reconcile himself to his imprudence—not such a bad lot after all:

> So, so; all friends! The wedding dinner cools,
> Who seem most crafty prove ofttimes most fools.   (V.ii. 206-207)

Thus, the Liberal position vindicates the wit who reaps the rewards, but it also manages to marry off the whore to a man who cannot object to her tarnished state. To have given "all" for love, therefore, need not mean total disaster. In her new, respectable status, the redeemed whore experiences an alteration of circumstances; the Liberal playwright presumes that her new situation will prompt a change of heart.

A Mad World, My Masters[7]

Though Middleton continues to prescribe marriage as the restorative for the drab's ills, the cure for the quean in *A Mad World, My Masters* proves to be a more charitable and just one than is found in the real world. The careless justice—which, in *A Trick to Catch the Old One*, rewards the Courtesan Jane with the "hand-me-down" Hoard, and the wit, Witgood, with the wealthy and virtuous Joyce—in *A Mad World, My Masters*, it is tidied up, and the courtesan Frank Gullman marries Follywit, the wit.

Young gallants like Witgood and Follywit cannot get their hands on their inheritance when they are young and need much for their riotous living, and the resistance on the part of their elders to part with this money before it is due gives rise to much of the scheming. As gallants, their code calls for good living in their youth and allows the future to fend for itself. In *A Mad World, My Masters,* Follywit immediately alerts us to his dilemma: "You all know the possibilities of my hereafter fortunes, and the humor of my frolic grandsire, Sir Bounteous Progress, whose death makes all possible to me: I shall have all when he has nothing; but now he has all, I shall have nothing. . . . They cannot abide to see us merry all the while they're above ground. . ." (I.i. 38-47).[8] Dick Follywit schemes to appropriate a portion of his inheritance prematurely and illegitimately: "What I take, then,/Is but a borrowing of so much beforehand" (II.ii. 35-36). He rationalizes that Sir Bounteous made his money as a usurer, and such capitalistic cunning, unacceptable to the gallant, smacks of puritan enterprise: "I am sure my grandsire ne'er got his money worse in his life than I got it from him. . . . Let the usurer look for't; for craft recoils in the end, . . ." (III.iii. 5-10).

His grandsire[9] certainly holds Follywit "at hard meat" (II.ii. 32), and his tight-fistedness rouses rebellion in his grandson: "Let sires and grandsires keep us low, we must/Live when they're flesh as well as when they're dust" (II.ii. 43-44). However, the generosity, geniality, and vitality with which Sir Bounteous is infinitely supplied makes him an eminently attractive character. The old knight maintains a very generous household, and if there is a fault to be found with him, it may be in his deference to the aristocracy, in spite of his wealth. Follywit is quick to note that Sir Bounteous "thinks himself never happier than when some stiff lord or great countess alights to make light his dishes" (I.i. 64-66). The fact that this old man keeps a courtesan and can permit himself the luxury of assuming that he has fathered a child, attests to his raffishness, high spirits and optimism. That he is impotent[10] in no way negates his reckless optimism and his unbounded self-confidence. Such a rakish grandsire seems a proper progenitor for the gallant Follywit. High among his accomplishments, Sir Bounteous gives recognition to Follywit's possession of "a good wit" (II.i. 134).

As a true gallant, Follywit sets much store by his wit, much as Witgood perceived it. Follywit prides himself on his leadership, cleverness, and craft which is all subsumed in his wit. Deciding that he can now gull "without conscience" and "without mercy" (I.i. 20-22), he prepares a plan to rob his grandsire. Ever the gallant and the trickster, Follywit is proud of his roguery, and his honor as a wit is sometimes more important to him than life itself. Disguised as a lord during one of his attempts to rob Sir Bounteous, he is so caught up with his role as "Master of the Revels," that he informs his fellow-conspirators he is willing to risk all: "I'll not have the jest spoil'd, that's certain, though it hazard a windpipe. I'll either go like a lord as I came, or be hang'd like a thief as I am; and that's my resolution" (II.iv. 88-91). One cannot help but admire the gallant's courage and to enjoy his knavishness. And Middleton veers oftener toward wit rather than virtue. The tone is thus set for the innumerable ironies which are the warp and woof of the comedy and create its holiday atmosphere. Follywit's craft and ingenuity to rob Sir Bounteous continue to meet with success.

However, when Follywit discovers that the old knight keeps a quean, he becomes convinced that she threatens his inheritance: "She carries away the thirds at least. 'Twill prove entail'd land, I am afraid, when all's done, i'faith. . . . Nay, I have known a vicious old, thought-acting father,/Damned only in his dreams, thirsting for game/(When his best parts hung down their heads for shame)/For his blanch'd harlot disposses his son/and make the pox his heir; . . ." (III.iii. 34-40). Convinced that his fears are not groundless, he devises a plan to dress up as a woman and impersonate Frank Gullman. Detailing his design, he contemplates the garments he will wear and discusses this with his comrade Mawworm: "Why, the doublet serves as well as the best, and is most in fashion. We're all male to th' middle, mankind from the beaver to the bum.[11] 'Tis an Amazonian time; you shall have women shortly tread their husbands" (III.iii. 103-105). Follywit seems fearful that women will dominate their husbands.[12]

As Follywit dresses for his part as the courtesan, his clowning acquaints us with some of the shoddy haunts in the Jacobean world of prostitution. He and Mawworm discuss brothels, their customers, and their rates.

Correctly attired and posing as Frank Gullman, Follywit must first contend with Sir Bounteous's man, Gunwater, before gaining admittance.   Vexed by his demeaning encounter with his grandsire's man, Follywit berates his grandsire: "Oh fie, in your crinkling days, grandsire, keep a courtesan to hinder your grandchild!" (IV.iii. 44-45). And in his final burst of peevishness, he cannot resist the usual harangue against harlotry: "Who keeps a harlot, tell him this from me,/He needs nor thief, disease, nor enemy" (49-50).

Though Follywit does not have a mistress, he is enough of a rake to be thoroughly acquainted with prostitution and brothels, judging from his conversation with Mawworm (III.iii.). Therefore, there is no need for such gratuituous mouthing of moralities sent forth either in pique to discredit Sir Bounteous, or possibly to allay his own guilt at his less-than-gallant behavior. It would seem that the whore continues to be the object of derision, disrespect and malevolence even by her most steadfast clients. When circumstantial evidence falsely convicts Frank Gullman as a jewel thief, and though Sir Bounteous still believes that she bears his child, he is quick to discredit her and to reveal his contempt for courtesans: "Is not a quean enough to answer for, but she must join a thief to 't? . . . A strumpet's love will have a waft i' th' end. . . . I ha' done, I ha' done, I ha' done with her, i'faith" (IV.iii. 83-104).

Such condemnation of the prostitute, however, does not influence Middleton sufficiently to paint an entirely unsympathetic portrait of the courtesan. Clever, quick, charming and resourceful, Frank Gullman is similar to Jane in *A Trick to Catch the Old One.* She plays her role honestly, allowing her adversary to trick himself so that she accomplishes her purpose. True, unlike Jane, Gullman is not an innocent girl who has been freshly seduced. But in a sense, she has had a greater burden to bear than the courtesan Jane. Gullman comes by her cozenage from a master. Middleton has seen fit to maker her mother her bawd.

Frank's mother boasts: "Fifteen times thou know'st I have sold thy maidenhead" (I.i. 149), and she by no means intends that the courtesan's career is over: "Though fifteen, all thy maidenheads are not gone./The Italian is not serv'd yet, nor the French;/The British men come for a dozen at once,/They engross all the market" (I.i. 156-159). The bawd's wisdom and advice to her daughter is a "how-to" on duplicity and deceit. She advises her to have "a sincere carriage, a religious eyebrow" (I.i. 161) so that she may thus charm "the worldings' senses" (162). Her mother's broad experience cautions the courtesan that sincerity and religious fervor have a special appeal for the debauched.[13] But ever anxious to make her daughter respectable she instructs her to be on the watch for a man who "honorable dotes" upon her, and if he is rich, to make certain to ensnare him as a husband. Though the bawd is acting in a crass, commercial manner, she still wants to see her daughter safely married. Thus, the bawd and the respectable parent both want to achieve the same end. Frank's mother's final tutelage embraces the wisdom that in a corrupt society appearances loom larger than reality:

> Be wisely tempered and learn this, my wench,
> Who gets th' opinin for a virtuous name
> May sin at pleasure, and ne'er think of shame. (I.i. 169)

While society requires chastity as the price of marriage for the female, Middleton's mad world knows the truth—the appearance is sufficient. The semblance of virtue gives one a license to transgress. The courtesan has evidently learned her lesson well for her reply is: "Mother, I am too deep a scholar grown/To learn my first rules now" (I.i. 170-171).

The sub-plot of *A Mad World, My Masters* is largely where the courtesan figures, and the appearance of virute, as opposed to the reality, operates as an important ingredient. The presence of Frank Gullman joins the plot and subplot in which Middleton presents us with Harebrain, the citizen, whose jealous "humour" makes him a candidate for cuckolding by Penitent Brothel, a "country gentleman." The courtesan, whom Harebrain supposes to be a virtuous matron, serves as a link in this adulterous liaison. Brothel's success with Mistress Harebrain is due largely to her husbands' foolishness, and a succubus appearing in the shape of Mistress Harebrain frightens both Penitent and his sexual partner into repentance.

Harebrain is cast in the same mold as Kitely in *Every Man in His Humour*. Puritanically-inclined, he lacks wit and is fair game for gulling. His own foolishness and distorted sexuality lead him into excessive behavior which guides his hand to help hammer in the horns. Not only is his perception of his wife's role twisted, but his judgment concerning Frank Gullman bears the same deformity since he is convinced that she is a "sweet virgin, the only companion his soul wishes for her [Mistress Harebrain]" (I.ii. 36-37). He counsels his spouse: "Wife, as thou lov'st the quiet of my breast,/ Embrace her counsel, yield to her advices" (I.ii. 148-149). He locks up his wife and she discloses to the courtesan how his jealousy makes prisoners of them both. Harebrain, continuing in his path of self-destruction, confides to the courtesan that he has censored all his wife's reading matter. He considers "Hero and Leander," and "Venus and Adonis" wanton pamphlets for a young married wife. Instead, Harebrain insists that she read the *Resolution,* which emphasizes the terrifying punishments the adulteress will undergo in hell, and also, he asks Gullman to enlarge on how loathsome is the life of a courtesan. Harebrain's thoughts, therefore, reflect the ideas of the society—a courtesan and an adulteress are really indistinguishable. The courtesan's *aside* heightens the comedy: "The gentleman would persuade me in time to disgrace myself, and speak ill of mine own function" (I.ii. 54-55).

Frank Gullman takes the business of converting Mistress Harebrain into an adulteress quite seriously and conscientiously applies herself to the task. Paying strict heed to her mother's teachings, the courtesan instructs Mistress Harebrain how to dissemble, to enjoy erotica, and still remain an "honest" wife:

> If he chance steal upon you, let him find
> Some book lie open 'gainst an unchaste mind,
> And coted scriptures, though for your own pleasure

> You read some stirring pamphlet, and convey it
> Under your skirt, the fittest place to lay it. (I.ii. 86-90)

The neat irony that Middleton employs makes Harebrain the perfect prey for his own senseless schemes. When the jealous husband insists upon rewarding the courtesan with a ruby for her "pains and counsel" in insuring his wife's purity, she protests to him with perfect honesty (as the Courtesan Jane does to Hoard when he insists upon pursuing her as a rich widow): "It is not so much worth, sir. I am a very ill counselor, truly" (I.ii. 142). In his tunnel-vision jealousy, he discounts her honesty and insists: "Go to, I say" (143).

While the courtesan enjoys Harebrain's complete confidence, she is, simultaneously, working for his wife's lover, Penitent Brothel, to create opportunities for assignations for them. Penitent recognizes his moral infirmity. Intellectually, he is aware of his propensity for sin, but, emotionally, he is impotent: "But why in others do I check wild passions,/ And retain deadly follies in myself?" (I.i. 90-91). He berates Follywit for his rash and wanton behavior, yet for himself "soothe[s] up adulterous motions,/And such an appetite that I know damns me,/Yet willingly embrace it; love to Harebrain's wife" (I.i. 94-96). He reproaches himself for his attempts to make Harebrain a cuckold and for his use of the courtesan and her mother to advance his dubious strategies to seduce Mistress Harebrain. His final denigration is voiced: "I am arriv'd at the court of conscience! A courtesan! Oh admirable times!" (I.i. 125-126). Breast-beating Brothel, like Malheureux in *The Dutch Courtesan*, makes a mockery of honest morality. He is not a scoundrel; he is simply a flaccid, weak-willed fool.

To arrange a rendezvous for the adulterers, the courtesan plans to pretend sudden illness so that Mistress Harebrain will be compelled to visit her, and Penitent is to disguise himself as her physician. When Penitent doubts that she can simulate sudden sickness, she retorts:

. . . we can be sick when we have a mind t't, catch an ague with the

> wind of our fans, surfeit upon the rump of a lark, and bestow ten
> pound in physic upon 't; . . . 'Tis the easiest art and cunning for
> our sect to counterfeit sick, . . . for since we were made for a
> weak, imperfect creature, we can fit that best that we are made
> for.   (II.v. 28-35)

Her reply indicates the low esteem in which women were held.[14]
However, the courtesan's cunning, artifice and ability turn
to advantage the male stereotype of women. She implies that
women are cleverly making fun of the male in the war
of the sexes. The male's stereotype of the woman does not
exemplify the woman; the low esteem merely exists in
the mind of the male. Frank's reply signifies that she has worked
within the limitations society has placed upon her, but
it is actually men who are being gulled and held in low esteem
by women. But Penitent is appreciative of the courtesan's
cleverness and congratulates her on her ingenious maneuver
to bring his assignation to fruition: "The wit of man
waves and decreases soon/But women's wit is ever at full moon"
(III.ii. 159-160). And Penitent pours forth his praise for
Mistress Harebrain when she outwits her jealous husband: "Art
of ladies!/When plots are e'en past hope and hang their
head,/Set with a woman's hand, they thrive and spread" (III.ii.
244-246). Petty acts of betrayal coupled with indefatigable
persistence are often the inferior's form of manipulating a situation. Caught in an unequal power trap, the subject person's retaliation is that of a subversive—clever surreptitious
maneuvering—but rarely that of a revolutionary.

Penitent Brothel, after his hijinks with Mistress Harebrain, undergoes a total transformation. At the beginning
of the fourth act, Penitent makes a long speech full of remorse
and condemns adultery. After berating himself for his in-
continence and lust, he, nevertheless, tars all women with the
brush of bestiality:

> To dote on weakness, slime, corruption, woman!
> What is she, took asunder from her clothes?   (IV.i. 18-19)

At this point a succubus in the shape of Mistress Harebrain enters and dancing, tries to entice Penitent. She

mouths all the myths associated with female temptation:

> Rouse thy amorous thoughts and twine me;
> All my interest I resign thee.
> . . . .
> Where's thy lip, thy clip, thy fadom?
> . . . .
> Art a man? or dost abuse one?
> A love? and knowst not how to use one?
> Come, I'll teach thee.   (IV.i. 46-55)[15]

But Penitent Brothel resists and in a later scene he preaches to Mistress Harebrain about the wickedness of adultery. However, it is interesting to note that unlike *Measure for Measure,* in which Juliet must accept the greater share of guilt for her sexual relations with Claudio, Penitent, while admonishing Mistress Harebrain, accepts the guilt for both:[16]

> Forgive me, Mistress Harebrain, on whose soul
> The guilt hangs double,
> My lust and thy enticement; both I challenge,
> And therefore of due vengence it appear'd
> To none but me, to whom both sins inher'd.   (IV.iv. 50-54)

Thus, in an uncommonly liberal view, the seducer, rather than the adulteress, openly bears the brunt of the guilt; the foolish, jealous husband deserves and gets his cuckolding and unwittingly learns his lesson; the wife, released from her prison of jealousy, repents and needs no lover to fill out her existence.[17]

While the courtesan was conniving to insure the success of Penitent's affair, her own craft recoiled upon her. Nevertheless, Gullman's resourcefulness and acuity are in constant reserve, and she draws upon them in this instance. She manages to make the unannounced visit of Sir Bounteous, who is keeping her, benefit her. Seeing her ill, and Brothel playing physician, the old man's first thought is that she has got the plague. After his fears are allayed, Sir Bounteous, with misplaced confidence, assumes that he has fathered a

child: "Hark in thine ear, thou'rt breeding of young bones;
I am afraid I have got thee with child, i'faith" (III.ii.
38-39). Puffed with pride, but reluctant to reveal his relationship with his quean, the old knight pretends to Penitent that Frank is his ill kinswoman, and he instructs
the physician to give her the best care regardless of cost.
Still reveling in the thought of his unexpected virility,
he promises Frank: "Well, be of good cheer, wench; there's
gold for thee.—I have fitted her; an old knight and a cock
o' th' game still; I have not spurs for nothing, I see"
(III.ii. 72-78). His unwarranted pleasure, founded on a groundless masculinity, causes the courtesan to remark to Penitent:
"How soon he took occasion to slip into his own flattery,
soothing his own defect. He fears he has done that deed
which I ne'er fear'd to come from him in my life" (III.ii.
85-88). Frank Gullman does not trick Sir Bounteous Progress but allows him to trick himself, a device often employed by Middleton which permits the gulls to trap themselves.

Dick Follywit, thus far, has enjoyed the role of rake
with impunity, but Frank Gullman, bright and beautiful,
a superb poseur, finally foils the wit. She is a most capable
actress, and her chef d'oeuvre is impersonating a virtuous
maiden. Whether she triumphs because Follywit is so smitten with her, or her ingenuous, virginal behavior merely
whets Follywit's appetite, he is totally taken in by her.
One cannot discount the part her mother plays in this
intrigue. She readily supports Frank's reticent behavior by
recounting how timorous she is, and how fearful she is
of men. Her "peevish honor" has cost her many a rich
suitor. This would seem to be a coup for Frank since
Follywit is such an experienced gallant. For Follywit,
courtship, which the courtesan "will not endure," is "a
blossom, and often brings forth fruit in forty weeks"
(IV.v. 6-9). But in spite of her reluctance to be "courted,"
Follywit is ready to submit that he is in love with her.
The courtesan's mother is convinced that she has realized
her triumph and elatedly assures Frank that Follywit will
marry her: "Why, I durst pawn my life the gentleman
means no other but honest and pure love to thee. How
say you, sir?" (IV.v. 74-80). In a totally unexpected re-

versal, Follywit replies: "By my faith, not I, lady" (IV.v. 76),
and the bawd boldly protests:

> Hark you there? What think you now, forsooth?
> What grieves your honor now?
> Or what lascivious breath intends to rear
> Against that maiden organ, your chaste ear?   (IV.v. 77-80)

In the very last words of the speech she continues to cleverly
connive. She encourages Follywit to pursue his suit by
telling him that she has persuaded Gullman to view Follywit advantageously. Perhaps a *double-entendre* is also intended. Follywit does not respond to the *double-entendre,*
but to the honest implication that the mother has prepared her daughter for his proposal. And the positive outcome of the deception results in Follywit's immediate
response with an honest marriage proposal. Much in the
fashion of the other gulls, Follywit discounts the bawd's
words and tricks himself. The mother is quick to recover
and promptly suggests: "Send for a priest and clap't up
within the hour" (IV.v. 108). They are wed. In spite of
Follywit's stellar performance, Frank Gullman's "virginal
innocence" wins the day. Follywit can now support his
claim to the first half of his name.

To deepen the irony, Dick confesses that his present
estate is poor but all will change when his grandsire dies.
He mentions that Sir Bounteous is "given to women; he
keeps a quean at this present," but he begs his mother-
in-law, "Do not tell my wife on 't" (IV.v. 117-118). The
bawd replies: "That were needless, i'faith" (121).

The mother rejoices in the marriage: "Thou'st wedded
youth and strength, and wealth will fall./Last, thou'rt
made honest" (IV.v. 138-139). And the courtesan's reply
proves that marriage, which gives her respectability, is
the most precious reward: "And that's worth 'em all"
(140).

The curtain comes down on a play which ends with
total forgiveness and rich blessings. It exalts acceptance,

tolerance and compassion. Rogues, hypocrites and fools are part of the human circus. It merely admits that men, all Adams like Overdo in *Bartholomew Fair,* never quite escape their flesh, blood, and folly. In *Bartholomew Fair,* Quarlous, the wit, who appears to be the spokesman for the values of the play personified in its mad world, testifies to Jonson's Cavalier code—he implies that we must take what we can get without being too morally fastidious. Though Quarlous loses Grace, he accepts his fortune from Dame Purecraft since it is money he wants. However, Middleton's Liberal approach in *A Mad World, My Masters,* represents a willingness to compromise and accept the world on its terms; it is lacking in the harsher, more careless morality which typifies the Cavalier vision.

Follywit, the wit, not unlike Quarlous, also wants gold, but he tempers his desires: he wants only what is rightly due him—a little in advance of the due date. Follywit is tricked into marrying a whore, but he does love her: "By my troth, she is as good a cup of nectar as any bachelor needs to sup at" (V.ii. 265-266). Aware now that the courtesan and her mother have deluded him, and that his chaste wife is his grandsire's ex-quean, he is willing to accept gold as indemnity for his loss: "Tut, give me gold, it makes amends for vice" (V.ii. 267). And Sir Bounteous Progress, cured of his lechery, and content that Follywit has been foiled, agrees, "This makes amends for all" (V.ii. 251). Follywit is engaging and accepts his courtesan, as well as his own follies, with good grace: "Tricks are repaid, I see" (V.ii. 261). He has, however, in spite of his imprudence, achieved his goal: he got his thousand marks as a dowry; he has also gained a winning, witty woman.

The courtesan has pledged to reform and to be a good wife: "What I have been is past; be that forgiven,/ And have a soul true both to thee and heaven" (V.ii. 259-260). The courtesan has found a haven in marriage, and her honesty need not be doubted, for she has been tested. Unaware that her husband Follywit is the actor in *The Slip,* she cries: "O' my troth, and I were not married I could find in my heart to fall in love with that player now, and send for him to a supper" (V.ii. 30-32). But she does not yield to this temptation—she remains faithful to Follywit. Her wish to wipe out her past and to redeem herself is further manifested when Follywit is caught stealing his grandsire's alarm-watch. Her fear is genuine when she cries: "Oh destiny! Have I married a thief, mother?" (V.ii. 231).

Follywit, too, has promised Sir Bounteous that in his new responsible state he will change his ways: ". . . you may be seriously assured of my hereafter stableness of life, I have took another course" (V.ii. 242-243). However, if his grandsire is an augury of Follywit's future, a flawless concord of wit and waggery may continue to be Follywit's legacy.

Middleton's Liberal approach to the puritanically-inclined Penitent and Harebrain continues to resemble the treatment accorded them by the Cavalier dramatists—they are humorous butts and their foolish excesses arouse only amusement. But his view of the quean's quandary, unlike that of the Cavalier's, clings to marriage as the resolution of her predicament. In *A Mad World, My Masters,* the prescription of marriage for Frank to the handsome, wealthy wit clearly cures the ills of her past and is the harbinger of a bright future. In a mad world, far more humane than the real world, such a satisfactory solution for the drab's dilemma is just. But in a less forgiving, sane society, such as in *A Trick to Catch the Old One,* the whore's husband is less likely to be the wit and more likely to be the flawed male.

Michaelmas Term[18]

As in *A Trick to Catch the Old One* and *A Mad World, My Masters,* marriage attempts to heal the pain of prostitution for the harlot in the sub-plot of *Michaelmas Term.* This play lacks the holiday quality and clemency of *A Mad World, My Masters.* The Country Wench, less sympathetically portrayed than either Jane or Frank Gullman, is subject to a sterner justice and marries the unsavory social climber. There is a movement in *Michaelmas Term* toward a more serious moral tone as Middleton decries prostitution and its practitioners more explicitly.

The plots are connected through Lethe's double life—his courtship of Quomodo's daughter in the main plot, and his keeping the courtesan in the sub-plot, with which we shall be largely concerned. In the sub-plot, Middleton deals mainly with two major themes: Lethe and his harlot's need to bury their identity in order to attain upward mobility; and the effects of prostitution on its practitioners. Master Andrew Lethe is "a gentleman of most received parts,/Forgetfulness, lust, impudence, and falsehood," notes Rearage, his rival for Quomodo's daughter; but even more important, he possesses the most unpardonable quality in comedy—"To wit, no wit at all" (I.i. 152-154).[19] His anxiety to overcome his base beginning as Wa'ter Gruel, son of a toothdrawer, and to pretend to be a City gallant, leads only to negation and a lack of identity which his rival Rearage is quick to discern. One of the gallants asks if Wa'ter Gruel "pass[es] for Lethe?" (I.i. 147), and Rearage retorts: "That no more know him than he knows himself" (I.i. 149).[20] Lethe, donning the clothes and affecting the behavior of a courtier, finds difficulty in distinguishing the appearance from the reality. Reminded that he has supped with the gallants yesterday, he affects a loss of memory:

> O, cry you mercy, 'tis so long ago,
> I had quite forgot you; I must be forgiven.
> Acquaintance, dear society, suits, and things
> Do so flow to me,
> That had I not the better memory,
> 'Twould be a wonder I should know myself.   (I.i. 166-171)

Lethe, who may know himself, has much difficulty judging others. His assessment of reality and of character is distorted by his own misshapen morality and materialism. Since Quomodo and his daughter both favor his suit, he cannot comprehend why Mistress Thomasine, the mother, is opposed to him. Since he is successful in "sudden fortunes" and has friends at court, Lethe's misguided conclusion is that Mistress Thomasine is in love with him "and would rather preserve [him] as a private friend to her own pleasures" (I.i. 209-211). Certain of his own superiority and sagacity, he writes to assure her that "by the marriage of your daughter I have the better means and opportunity to yourself, and without the least suspicion" (I.i. 221-222). Thomasine can, of course, only be scornful of such "a base, proud knave" (II.iii. 9), for she has not forgotten "how he came up" (9), and is not taken in by his appearance. Dressed in his white satin suit he appears to her "like a maggot crept out of a nutshell, a fair body and a foul neck" (II.iii. 13-14), and "for all his cleansing, pruning, and paring, he's not worthy a broker's daughter" (II.iii. 15-16).

To relieve her loneliness, Lethe's widowed mother has come to look for her son, and in a chance meeting he is fearful that she will recognize him and betray his true identity:

> My mother! Curse of poverty! Does she come up to shame me, to betray my birth, and cast soil upon my new suit? Let her pass me, I'll take no notice of her. (I.i. 236-238)

His mother, however, does not recognize him in his new raiment. When he says, "Know you not me, good woman?" (I.i. 261), she replies: "Alas, an't please your worship, I never saw such a glorious suit since the hour I was kersen'd" (264). Delighted that he has successfully submerged his true identity by his appearance, he decides to employ his mother as his bawd: "I may employ her as a private drudge/To pass my letters and secure my lust" (I.i. 268-269). In *Michaelmas Term,* the bawd is now mother to the son and will adopt the role of student rather than that of teacher.

Lethe gives Mother Gruel sixpence but insists that she maintain her distance. When she protests that she is "a clean old woman," his explanation makes a mockery of honest values: "It goes not by cleanness here, good woman; if you were fouler, so you were braver [more richly dressed], you might come nearer" (I.i. 296-297). Citing the conversation I have noted, Brian Gibbons observes: "A scene between a plain honest mother and her vicious, materialistic son makes a firm didactic point about the dehumanization by urban evil of the prodigal Lethe."[21] However, the mother's reply does create some doubt about her plain honesty:

> Nay, and that be the fashion, I hope that I shall get it shortly; there's no woman so old but she may learn, and as an old lady delights in a young page or monkey, so there are young courtiers will be hungry upon an old woman, I warrant you.
> (I.i. 298-301)

His mother's statement implies that she is not "such a simple old woman," and she seems to be a willing student who is ready to accommodate herself to prostitution with ease. Perhaps the implication is that Lethe's ignoble instincts may have had their roots in his base beginnings, but even if she had been honest up to this point, she is corruptible. Such a view would tend to corroborate Middleton's concept that depravity is ever in fashion and that all women have a predilection for wantonness.

While Lethe's mother unknowingly serves as his bawd, he retain Dick Hellgill, a pandar, "to look out some third sister[22] or entice some discontented gentlewoman from her husband, whom the laying out of [his] appetite shall maintain" (I.i. 225-228). Lethe promises them: "I'll keep you in good fashion, ladies; no meaner men than knights shall ransom home your gowns and recover your smocks; I'll not dally with you" (I.i. 231-233). Lethe, fast learning to be a "gentleman," is quick to pick up the disreputable ways of the gallant—his sexual trafficking will exploit the discontent of women, and he will thus introduce them to prostitution.

Hellgill, commissioned to procure a prostitute for Lethe, entices the gullible Country Wench from her father with the lure of large satisfactions in the City. She remonstrates with him:

Country Wench: Why did you entice me from my father?

Hellgill: Why? To thy better advancement. Would'st
              thou, a pretty, beautiful, juicy squall, live in a
              poor thrum'd house i' th' country in such servile
              habilments, and may well pass for a gentlewoman
              i' th' city? Does not five hundred do so, think'st
              thou, and with worse faces?   (I.ii. 3-7)

Suggested in Hellgill's lure is the pandering to her social aspirations (acting the part of a lady as a mistress or wife) as well as
the intimation that prostitution is an accepted method for females to get ahead.[23]   Since the Country Wench is still a little
fearful of the big City and defloration, the procurer offers her
encouragement: "Yet indeed 'tis the fashion of any courtesan
to be seasick i' th' first voyage, but at next she proclaims open
wars, like a beaten soldier. Why Northamptonshire lass, dost
dream of virginity now?" (9-12). Persisting, Hellgill heartens the
wench, emphasizing how clothes will enable her to pass as a
gentlewoman, a form of deception practiced by the social climber Lethe. Hellgill enumerates the varieties of disguises available
to her: "Wires and tires, bents and bums, felts and falls, thou
shalt deceive the world, that gentlewomen shall not be known
from others" (I.ii. 13-15).[24]   The lengthy, uplifting address ends
with a soupçon of Middleton's keen irony: "I have a master to
whom I must prefer thee after the aforesaid decking, Lethe by
name, a man of one most admired property: he can both love
thee, and for thy better advancement be thy pander himself, an
exc'llent spark of humility" (I.ii. 15-19).

    Sensuality plays no part in the Country Wench's motive to
sin; it is her intense desire for advancement that persuades her
to consider prostitution as a means. However, still dubious,
fearful and guilt-ridden, but sorely tempted, she blames the
pander for catering to her wickedness: "Well, heaven forgive
you, you train me to 't. . . . If I had not a desire to go like a
gentlewoman, you should be hang'd ere you should get me to
't, I warrant you" (I.ii. 20, 27-28). But Dick's skeptical reply
merely indicates his disbelief and his low esteem of the entire
female sex:

> I know you are all chaste enough,
> Till one thing or another tempt you!
> Deny a satin gown and you dare now?   (I.ii. 31-33)

And the pander persists in his role as tempter: he appeals to the wench's weakness for finery. In her hierarchy of values, the Country Wench's penchant for rich apparel outranks virginity. But finery denotes more than mere adornment or cosmetic appeal. It has a greater value for her—rich raiment is synonymous with living the life of a lady, and to her simple way of thinking she fantasizes that as a caparisoned courtesan she will establish a new identity as a lady, a state which could never be hers at home in the country with her father. The procurer, now brusque and businesslike, makes her anticipated role clear to her:

> Virginity is no city trade,
> You're out o' th' freedom, (city limits)
>   when you're a maid;
> . . . .
>   thou art fair and fresh,
> The gilded flies will light upon thy flesh.   (II.i. 43-48)[25]

But the Country Wench cannot see the trap which is being laid for her. All her resistance is gone and she crumbles: "Beshrew your sweet enchantments, you have won" (49). Hellgill, both triumphant and contemptuous of her, gloats:

> How easily soft women are undone.
> So farewell wholesome weeds, where treasure pants,
> And welcome silks, where lies disease and wants.—   (II.i. 51-53)

The procurer's *aside* reinforces the depravity and ills of prostitution and how the wench is trading true happiness for frippery. All indecision and fears resolved, the girl brushes whoredom from her mind; instead, she looks forward only to the glories that will accrue to her in her new state: "I am in a swoon till I be a gentlewoman" (II.i. 55-56). Though innocent of the ways of the world, the wench is firmly convinced that prostitution is her one opportunity for upward mobility and large satisfactions. In her farewell note to her father she explicitly mentions that she has contemplated such a move for a long time:

> Father, wonder not at my so sudden departure, without your leave
> or knowledge . . . had you had knowledge of it, I know you would

have sought to restrain it, and hinder me from what I have long desir'd. Being now happily prefer'd to a gentleman's service in London, about Holborn, if you please to send, you may hear well of me.   (II.ii. 9-15)

When the pander prepares Lethe for meeting his "delicate piece of sin" (II.i. 136), lowly-born Lethe's ironical comment is: "Of what parentage?" (II.i. 137). Hellgill's lying retort makes her "a gentlewoman of a great house" (138), and his *aside* mocks both social climbers, but comes down harder on him: "She newly come out of a barn, yet too good for a toothdrawer's son" (II.i. 140-141). Though Andrew Lethe's sexual preferences lean toward the wife rather than the maid—"Oh, adultery is a great deal sweeter/In my mind" (143-144)—he accepts the girl. Both Andrew and Dick discuss the Country Wench in terms of a commodity and the pander demands his broker's fee for this purchase: "Her firstlings shall be mine,/Swine look but for the husks; the meat be thine" (II.i. 148-149).[26]

Set up in lodgings and fashionably dressed, the courtesan appears at the beginning of the third act as a newly installed member of the oldest profession. Harping on her heritage and pretension, Dick Hellgill greets her: "What base birth does not raiment make glorious?" (III.i. 1-2). He then generalizes that all women are deceivers: "Why should not a woman confess what she is now, since the finest are but deluding shadows, begot between tirewoman and tailors?" (3-5). The procurer continues to rip away at the wench's disguise and to lay bare her rustic origins: "Who would think now this fine sophisticated squall came out of the bosom of a barn, and the loins of a haytosser?" (III.i. 22-23). But the courtesan will not permit the pander to strip away the new identity she has purchased so dearly: "Out, you saucy, pestiferous pander! I scorn that, i'faith" (24). Dick can only characterize her disavowal as the mark of her trade: "Excellent, already the true phrase and style of a strumpet" (25). When the pander continues to taunt her in this vein and comments that her own father would scarcely know her, the courtesan then begins to realize that she has traded her identity for this shallow existence, for the fantasy of playing a lady's role—scarcely the reality. She comments: "How can he [her father] know me, when I scarce know myself?" (30-31). But prostitution with its sham and superficial glitter has captured her. Her father, concerned with her whereabouts, comes to London, disguised, to look for her. He works for her, and ironically, neither ever recognizes the other. In a sermonlike soliloquy, he warns young women of the pitfalls of the big City, similar to Bellafront's father, Friscobaldo, in *The Honest Whore, Part II*, who talks of his "dear and only daughter" (II.ii. 5).[27] Friscobaldo, who had long ago repented of his "unshapen youth" (II.ii. 22) and "swinish riots" (24),[28] also feared for his daughter's honor. Acting as a moral chorus, the Country Wench's father has but little effect. Engaged to serve his courtesan daughter, he does not recognize her in her finery and mistakes her for a lady; similarly, Mother Gruel mistakes her son for a gentleman. Middleton's neat irony is apparent as the father appraises his daughter:

> A mistress of a choice beauty! Amongst such imperfect creatures
> I ha' not seen a perfecter; I should have reckoned the fortunes of
> my daughter amongst the happiest, had she lighted into such a
> service. . . .   (III.i. 54-57)

The father is still present as Lethe, pleased with his courtesan, introduces her to his gallants as "a gentlewoman of a great house, noble parentage, unmatchable education" (III.i. 73-74). Then in a complete reversal, unmatched for cockiness and base behavior, he humiliates her: "I may grace her with the name of a courtesan, a backslider, a prostitute or such a toy; but when all comes to all, 'tis but a plain pung [punk] " (III.i. 74-77). But the wench has quickly learned that the prostitute has not the privilege of pride, and contemptuous cuts must be met with ardent expressions: "Oh, my beloved strayer! I consume in thy absence" (79).

The courtesan's parent, privy to all the commotion, begins to realize that his mistress scarcely meets the specifications of a lady: "But I scarce like my mistress now; the loins/Can ne'er be safe where the flies be so busy" (III.i. 108-109). During the same encounter, the Country Wench learns that Lethe is courting Quomodo's daughter. She jealously lashes out and threatens him:

> Do you deceive me so? Are you toward marriage, i'faith
> Master Lethe? It shall go hard but I'll forbid the banes [banns] ;

> I'll send a messenger into your bones, another
> into your purse, but I'll do 't.   (III.i. 255-258)

Though the wench's malevolence does not envision murder (merely syphilis and poverty), it bears the same pernicious spirit which arouses the Dutch Courtesan to violence after she has been spurned by Freevill. But both the Country Wench and the Dutch Courtesan, as well as the "honest whore," are emotionally involved with just one man, and they do not envision themselves as common prostitutes, however self-deluding this may be. They have a more benevolent view of themselves than is held by the man with whom they believe they have a singular attachment. Consequently, if they do not perceive themselves as garden-variety whores, they are, at least, aspiring to the situation of a permanently-kept mistress—a courtesan with a constant lover.

At this point, the father bursts all restraint, and his condemnation of prostitution assumes a very serious moralizing quality. Middleton's castigation of whoredom enunciates a more didactic Puritanical stance, unlike his other two comedies, and it more closely resembles the tone of *The Honest Whore:*

> Thou fair and wicked creature, steeped in art,
> Beauteous and fresh, the soul the foulest part!   (III.i. 259-260)

Aware that he is a bawd to a prostitute, he voices his horror: "To be bawd!/Hell has not such an office" (IV.ii. 3). When he chastizes the Country Wench for the wickedness of her trade, the courtesan rebukes him and, in a mildly ironic manner, she reproaches him for his sanctimonious attitude and essentially defends prostitution with a rather cheerful flippancy. She considers her trade as honest as the merchant's. Both are accepted practice, she claims:

> Do not all trades live by their ware, and yet call'd honest livers?
> Do they not thrive best when they utter most, and make it away
> by the great? Is not wholesale the chiefest merchandise? . . .
> You're foully deceiv'd and you think so.   (IV.ii. 10-16)[29]

But the whore's flippancy is severely undercut when the father's sharp retort continues to excoriate her for her whorish behavior:

> You are so glu'd to punishment and shame
> Your words e'en deserve whipping.
> To bear the habit of a gentlewoman,
> And be in mind so distant!   (IV.ii. 17-20)

Instead of compelling the courtesan to examine her conduct and repent, the moralizing merely irritates her. She is now thoroughly steeped in the way of sin; being a prostitute in the City has made her cynical. With self-righteous brutality, she inveighs against gentlewomen:

> Why, you fool you, are not gentlewomen sinners? And there's no courageous sinner amongst us, but was a gentlewoman by the mother's side, I warrant you. Besides, we are not always bound to think those our fathers that marry our mothers, but those that lie with our mothers, and they may be gentlemen born, and born again, for ought we know, you know.   (IV.ii. 21-27)[30]

Signifying his impotence to reclaim the whore, and crushed by her rhetoric, the father's final remarks mouth Middleton's cynical view:

> True, corruption may well be generation's first;
> 'We're bad by nature, but by custom worst.'

While Middleton believes that the world is wicked and corruption and sin are still rampant, *Michaelmas Term* indicates a tendency toward moral responsibility, even in a universe which does not always reward the virtuous and punish the wicked. In both *A Trick to Catch the Old One* and *A Mad World, My Masters,* immorality and sin are diluted in lenience and laughter. But Middleton adopts a more serious stance in *Michaelmas Term* and points up the moral flaw.

The themes of social climbing and sex are also exploited in the main plot. The tug of war between the aristocracy and the middle class is symbolized largely in the areas of property and sex. Quomodo, a merchant, in the style of Hoard and Lucre, is concerned to extend his property. Unlike the complacent gentry, Middle-class Quomodo means to get this land by his wits, whether licitly or illicitly. He is a hypocritical puritan with marketplace attitudes who is willing to prostitute even his own wife, Thomasine, as evidenced by his remark to his henchman, Shortyard:

> There are means and ways enow to hook in gentry,
> Besides our deadly enmity, which thus stands:
> They're busy 'bout our wives, we 'bout their lands.   (I.i. 105-107)

Shortyard quickly perceives that Quomodo is willing to risk even the loathsome prospect of cuckoldry to gain land.

The one redemptive feature in the play is Thomasine, whom Quomodo is so willing to reduce to a commodity. Mirrored in Middleton's depiction of Thomasine and the Country Wench is a thematic connection between main and sub-plot concerning female independence. Thomasine is drawn as a morally strong, autonomous individual whom Middleton treats with genuine respect. The Country Wench, on the other hand, is regarded as having moral sloth and appears as a piece of property looking for a purchaser. Both are sovereign women, but Thomasine's character is sterling, the courtesan's tarnished. Thomasine is not the ordinary citizen's wife interested in clothes, carriages and gallants. Middleton treats her as a woman of independent mind and firm morality. When Quomodo successfully cheats Easy, Thomasine, looking on, can no longer stand by; instead she shows awareness that one is fully accountable to one's own conscience:

> Why stand I here (as late our graceless dames
> That found no eyes) to see that gentleman
> Alive, in state and credit, executed,
> Help to rip up himself, does all he can?
> Why am I wife to him that is no man?
> I suffer in that gentleman's confusion   (II.iii. 202-207)[31]

It is only then that Quomodo's wife compensates Easy with money. Though she is sympathetic toward Easy and attracted to him, no sexual relationship exists before their marriage. It is only after the wedding that she says: "I have the leisure now both to do that gentleman good and do myself a little pleasure" (IV.iii. 40-41). But when Quomodo rises from his feigned death, she is willing, however reluctantly, to leave Easy and return to him.

The play ends with a courtroom scene so that justice may be meted out. Lethe, of course, loses his rich virgin to the gentleman Rearage, for Lethe lacks a necessary ingredient—wit. Susan is alienated from him because she "loath[es] the sin he follows" (V.iii. 117), whoredom. Because of his "lust, impudence, and falsehood," he is treated as a clown and is fated to marry the whore. When Lethe, at first, refuses to marry her, the Country Wench puts forth her claim: "I crave it [marriage] on my knees; such was his vow at first" (V.iii. 103).[32] And the pander, to protect himself against being prodded into such a marriage, attests to her statement:

> (*Aside*) I'll say so too, and work out mine own safety.—
> Such was his vow at first, indeed, my lord,
> Howe'er his mood has chang'd him!   (V.iii. 104-106)

The Judge decrees: "He shall both marry and taste punishment" (V.iii. 108). Lethe's cynical comment then denotes the corruption of all women: "Marry a harlot, why not? 'Tis an honest man's fortune. I pray, did not one of my countrymen marry my sister? Why, well, then, if none should be married but those that are honest, where should a man seek a wife after Christmas?" (V.iii. 122-125).[33] Lethe requests of the Judge: "I do beseech your lordship to remove/The punishment [whipping] ;/I am content to marry her" (V.iii. 129-130). But the Judge insists that he shall be whipped, too, unless he is pardoned by his mother. She knows Andrew is a wicked son who has been corrupted and was more honest when he had "scarce a shirt" (V.iii. 162). Her summation of his character stresses the damge to his identity, his dissembling, and deception. There is no explicit pardon, but neither is there further mention of punishment for Lethe.

Michaelmas Term is a comedy; wit must still win out, but the gallants who succeed are not profligates. Easy is a gullible country gentleman who learns that the City is full of sin, and mends his ways, regaining his estate from Quomodo. Rearage, the gallant, it would seem, will turn away from his past, capricious behavior and love his wife, Quomodo's daughter, and her generous dowry.

Though Quomodo is the central intriguer and his tricks

produce merriment, his punishment is more severe than that of Hoard or Sir Bounteous. He loses not only the land he cozened, but he must live with the results of his unsavory conduct. Of Quomodo, the Judge declares: "Thou art thine own affliction" (V.iii. 164).

While the Country Wench is not as witty, resourceful and appealing as Jane and Frank Gullman, and her fantasies and dreams are short-lived, she does reflect the adventurous spirit of the times, and she risks security for a chance to rise in the world and to try to make a better life for herself. She chooses prostitution as a short-sighted means for achieving her ends and believes she is successful. In a period of transition and upheaval, and in keeping with the spirit of the times, it is often easier for lower class women to improve their social status. Many want to become "ladies." Thus, the country girl looks to the city to satisfy this longing, and virginity is generally her most marketable ware. Such is the route the Country Wench takes. Middleton portrays her with little sympathy: she does not proclaim her love for Lethe nor does she promise to reform.

In *Michaelmas Term*, Middleton's picture of the courtesan is harsher and his more serious, moral tone, and treament of prostitution seem to indicate a closer kinship with the Puritan dramatist Dekker. This affinity exists because Middleton authentically portrays the evils of harlotry with no pleasant laughter to dilute their impact. Lethe and the courtesan appear as unattractive characters, and Middleton rejects their assault on morality for the rewards of greater social gains. Middleton's analysis of prostitution has an ironic tone, and his emphasis is on the delusions and shoddiness of its trafficking.

While marriage without repentance still remains the Liberal dramatist's resolution for the whore's ills, there is less stress on magnanimity and merriment, and more movement toward accountability. Insofar as Lethe and the Country Wench are concerned, their marketplace morality deluded them into trading their old identity for a seemingly newer, more profitable one. But Middleton's movement toward accountability extracts a kind of poetic justice from their marriage—Lethe and the courtesan will have to live with each other, rather than with their delusion of what profit their new selves could bring.

NOTES

[1] Selecting T. S. Eliot's assertions as the pivotal point for this controversy—since his essay on Middleton in 1927 helped generate so much interest in the dramatist—see *Elizabethan Essays* (London: Faber & Faber, 1934), p. 89, where he terms Middleton "merely a name, a voice, the author of certain plays. . . . He has no point of view, is neither sentimental nor cynical; he is neither resigned, nor disillusioned nor romantic; he has no message. He is merely the name which associates six or seven great plays." However, it is also evident that Eliot broadens his attitude to include Middleton's depiction of women, which would indicate that he has some sort of "voice." Except for Shakespeare, Eliot asserts, p. 95, "Middleton understood woman in tragedy better than any of the Elizabethans— . . . he was also able, in his comedy, to present a finer woman than any of them." In trenchant disagreement are Arthur C. Kirsch, *Jacobean Dramatic Pespectives* (Charlottesville: University Press of Virginia, 1972), p. 75, who claims for Middleton a "powerful dramatic 'point of view'," and L. C. Knights, *Drama and Society in the Age of Jonson* (London: Chatto & Windus, 1951), p. 257, who places the greater stress on social changes. Brian Gibbons, *Jacobean City Comedy* (Cambridge, Massachusetts: Harvard University Press, 1968), p. 17, is generally in accord with Knights' economic concept. See Richard Levin in the introduction to his edition of *Michaelmas Term*, Regents Renaissance Drama Series (Lincoln, Nebraska, 1966), p. xv., and David M. Holmes, *The Art of Thomas Middleton* (Oxford: Clarendon Press, 1970), p. 25, who assert that Middleton remains a realist and a satirist. Alfred Harbage, *Shakespeare and the Rival Traditions* (New York: The Macmillan Company, 1952), p. 71, finds no morality in Middleton and rigorously condemns him with other "coterie" writers. Una Ellis-Fermor, *The Jacobean Drama*, 4th ed. rev. (London: Methuen & Company, Ltd., 1961), pp. 128-129, harmonizes with Eliot's theory and both would seem to vindicate Middleton of Harbage's harsh criticism that his dramas are lewd and tasteless. F. E. Schelling, *Elizabethan Playwrights* (New York: Benjamin Blom, 1965), p. 515, says Middleton saw life "as a man of the world . . . and not as the moralist presents it." Thomas M. Parrott and Robert H. Ball, *A Short View of Elizabethan Drama* (New York: Charles Scribner's Sons, 1958), p. 170, reaffirm this conviction. Anthony Covatta, *Thomas Middleton's City Comedies* (Lewisburg; Bucknell University Press, 1973), whose concepts I find most in accord with my own, p. 46, denies Middleton's comedies are satiric; and on p. 53, he finds that Middleton's vision "is not antisocial but ultimately social . . . it reminds us of our all-too-human imperfection."

2Keith Thomas, "The Double Standard," *Journal of the History of Ideas,* 20 (1959), especially pp. 195-203, from an unpublished paper, "The Lady Doth Protest: Protest in the Popular Writings of Renaissance Englishwomen," by Dr. Betty Travitsky.

3Plot: Young Witgood, the hero, ruined by his riotous living and the usury of Lucre, his uncle, decides to cast off his mistress Jane and to marry the chaste, rich niece of his uncle's enemy and rival, Walkadine Hoard. Capitalizing on the feud between the two old rogues, each eager to gain the supposed wealth of the Courtesan posing as a rich widow, Witgood skillfully exploits them. His plan succeeds and he gets back the titles of his land from Lucre, has his debts paid by Hoard, and wins the hand of the rich maiden Joyce. Hoard, anxious to outwit Lucre, tricks himself; he marries the Courtesan.

4I am indebted to Leonora L. Brodwin for this view which is largely drawn from her analysis of *The Changeling,* in *Elizabethan Love Tragedy, 1587-1625* (New York University Press, 1971), pp. 151-153.

5This standard Cavalier attitude is treated at large in the sub-plot. Addressing himself to his servant, Audrey, he sprays her with a shower of invective: "Out, you blabiaminy; you unfeathered creamtoried quean; you cullisance of scabiosity" (IV.v. 52-53). Her mildly ironic retort: "Good words, Master Dampit, to speak before a maid and a virgin. . . . Sweet terms! My mistress shall know 'em" (54-57). Audrey, evidently posing as the innocent, is probably having sexual relations with her master, for she shortly says: "Pray, gentlemen, depart; his [Dampit's] hour's come upon him.—Sleep in my bosom, sleep (IV.v. 195-196). Meanings for some of the words he uses are footnoted by ed. Hazelton Spencer, in *Elizabethan Plays* (Lexington, Massachusetts: D. C. Heath & Company, 1933), as follows: p. 1010 "Blabiaminy"-Babbler; "Unfeathered creamatoried"-Burnt, syphilitic (Kittridge)—"unfeathered" implies that she has lost her hair from the pox; Footnote 68-Cullisance-a corruption of "cognizane"-badge.

When Hoard invites Dampit to his wedding dinner with "A rich widow" (IV.v. 154), Dampit repeats it as "A Dutch widow" (155) which was synonymous with prostitute," noted in Footnote, p. 1011. Hoard then clarifies his statement: "A rich widow; one Widow Medler" (156), and Dampit again distorts it: "Medler? She keeps open house" (157). Footnote, p. 1011 notes that another name for medlar, the fruit, was "openarse."

6While Covatta highlights the "redemptive nature of Witgood's actions," p. 106, and compares him to Prince Hal in *Henry IV, Part I*, p. 113, Holmes sees in him "a rudimentary discovery of conscience and obligation," p. 82, and Price purports that he is repentant at the beginning of the play and reformed at the end, p. 136. Parrott and Ball believe, "The truth is that all Middleton's sympathy goes out to the clever young rogue who has outwitted the old one," p. 161. While Middleton's view may be more dispassionate and less inclined to indicate sympathy, it assuredly sees the world from an amoral vantage point when, in the last analysis, the wit wins all he wishes.

[7]Plot: This play's plot resembles that of *A Trick to Catch the Old One* in basic detail. Follywit, too, is a gallant who needs money, and his campaign against his grandsire, Sir Bounteous Progress, is his revenge on an elder who has promised him his estate but refuses to part with any part of it before he dies. In a series of disguises and intrigues, Follywit outwits the lively, genial old man of some considerable sums of money.

Frank Gullman, the mistress of Sir Bounteous, whose mother is her bawd, lets a jealous husband, Harebrain, persuade himself of her purity. In turn, she is asked to set an example of virtue for Harebrain's wife. In this role she arouses Mistress Harebrain's passion for Penitent Brothel and arranges their assignations. Gullman also permits Sir Bounteous to trick himself into thinking that she is pregnant with his child which proves lucrative for her. In her role as chaste maiden, she convinces Follywit that she is a virgin, and they marry. Follywit then learns that he has married Sir Bounteous's mistress, but all are reconciled and to sweeten the defeat, his grandsire gives Follywit money.

[8]*Thomas Middleton: A Mad World, My Masters,* ed. Standish Henning (Lincoln: University of Nebraska Press, 1965). All further references are to this edition.

[9]See listing in "The Actors in the Comedy" of edition used. Richard Follywit is listed as "nephew to Sir Bounteous Progress," but he is referred to as his "grandson," and Sir Bounteous is called his "grandsire."

[10]Sir Bounteous's impotence is hinted at early in the play by the courtesan's mother. Though Frank Gullman is no longer a virgin, her mother notes: "There's maidenhead enough for old Sir Bounteous still,/ He'll be all his lifetime about it yet,/And be as far to seek when he has done" (I.i. 151-153). At the end of the play the courtesan makes a similar comment: "Give me your hand, sir; you ne'er yet begun with me" (V.i. 104).

[11]Henning, p. 61, notes that "beaver to the bum" is "hat to the waist." See Camden, p. 221, who explains that women often wore doublets which were almost duplicates of those worn by men. This encroachment on male style was severely criticized by Gascoigne, Stubbes, Greene and other male writers. See also James T. Henke, *Courtesans and Cuckolds* (New York: Garland Publishing Company, 1979), p. 30, who lists "Bum" as "Anus."

[12]Actually, there was a group of London "feminists" in Jacobean society who wore men's clothes, carried weapons, and created a furor. Though this form of dress appears to have started in about the 1580s, these women came in for sharp criticism by the monarch, pulpit and press from about 1600 to 1620. The donning of male attire caused much open debate between women and the men who condemned them. These early feminine activists raised the male/female issues regarding social stereotypes and male domination.

    See also Mary Frith. "Frith, Mary." *Dictionary of National Biography,* ed. Leslie Stephen and Sidney Lee (London: Oxford University Press, 1921-1922), 7, 720-721, who lived 1584?-1659 and exemplified the "feminist" woman. According to her anonymous biographer, she was well educated but spurned any type of household work and dressed as a man. She is the heroine of a comedy, "The Roaring Girle," 1611, by Middleton and Dekker. See also E. K. Chambers, "Elizabethan Stage Gleaning," *Review of English Studies,* 1 (January, 1925), 77-78, who confirms that she wore boots with a sword at her side, went to taverns, tobacco shops and to plays. For her unconventional dress and behavior, she was considered a disgrace to womanhood and served time in Bridewell. See also Camden, pp. 264-265, in which the writer John Trundle attacks the Man-Woman for her "shorne Hayre" and loose ways. The Man-Woman replies, sharply defending her sex and making a strong point about the need for women to be liberated from their confined clothes, as well as their need for freedom of choice and freedom to change.

[13]See *Measure for Measure* (II.ii. 168-186), in which Angelo states that it is Isabella's virtue, sincerity and purity which excite him sexually: "Can it be/That modesty may more betray our sense/Than woman's lightness?" (168-169).

[14]See Stone, p. 198. He notes that the "Homily on Marriage" was ordered to be read in church by the Crown every Sunday from 1562 on. It made very clear that women were considered inferior: "The woman is a weak creature not endued with like strength and constancy of mind: therefore, they be the soon disquieted, and they be the more prone to all weak affections and dispositions of mind, more than men be; and lighter they be, and more vain in their fantasies and opinions." While this referred to wives, there is no doubt that all women were looked upon as inferior to men.

[15]See note 23 in Introduction.

[16]Middleton's uncommon, avante-garde view of the guilt falling large-ly on Penitent attests to his realistic approach to the situation. He accepts the existence of immoral practices but looks at them in an objective man-ner. While women may entice men, Middleton seems aware that men will have the greater power over women, and it is generally they who are in a better position to pursue the woman in an extra-marital affair. Women at this time also began to protest the fact that men lure women "to fall" and then fault them for falling. It occurs in controversial literature between 1567 and 1640.

[17]See Leggatt, p. 138, who believes Middleton "attempts to combine the adultery intrigue with a more overt moral commentary." Were this so, the wife could not have escaped punishment, and all three would scarcely have "posed in a final tableau of forgiveness, love, and friendship." Such a forgiving, fun finale would seem an inappropriate conclusion for a "more overt moral commentary." See also Wilbur Dwight Dunkel, *The Dramatic Technique of Thomas Middleton in His Comedies of London Life* (New York: Russell & Russell, 1967), p. 54, where he asserts, "Harebrain seems to be the only person interested in chastity, and yet he is made ridiculous by his well-founded but unsympathetically represented, jealousy of his wife." However, this is also true of Penitent Brothel even though he falls. He is given unsympathetic treatment and is made to appear ridiculous.

[18]Plot: The main plot deals with Easy, a country gentleman, who comes to the city for Michaelmas Term and loses money at dice. Quomodo, a draper, with the aid of two apprentices, cozens Easy. In order to be re-leased from his debt, Easy gives Quomodo a bond for all his property. Quomodo's wife, Thomasine, strongly disapproves of her husband's conduct and falls in love with Easy. When Quomodo feigns death to test his family's grief and to spy on their spending habits, Thomasine marries Easy. Quomo-do comes back to life, is tricked into returning Easy's property, and is banished by the judge without wife or property. The main plot also deals with Rearage, a gentleman, and Lethe, an adventurer, who are rivals for Quomodo's daughter.

The sub-plot is concerned with Lethe and the Country Wench. Lethe uses his mother, who does not recognize him in his new city finery, as his bawd. His pander, Hellgill, secures the Country Wench by luring her to the city with promises of beautiful clothes. In her new trappings, the Country Wench's father, who comes to look for her, does not recognize her and takes service in her establishment, not unlike Lethe's mother. The father pleads with his daughter to give up her life of sin. Lethe and the Country Wench are caught in disgrace and he is forced to marry her.

[19]Thomas Middleton, *Michaelmas Term*, ed. Richard Levin (Lincoln:

University of Nebraska Press, 1966). All further references are to this edition.

[20]See Levin, Introduction, p. xiv, who notes that his assumed name refers to the river Lethe in Hades, denoting forgetfulness. This ties in with his need to obliterate all traces of his past in his new social-climbing role.

[21]Gibbons, p. 131.

[22]Levin, p. 18, notes explanation for "third sister": "Since daughters were often married off by seniority, a girl with two older unwed sisters might well despair of ever marrying (especially if, as Price suggests, the family cannot afford three dowries), and so be susceptible."

[23]The enticements the procurer uses indicate that the "country girl/ city slicker" routine has not changed in over three centuries. In the seventeenth century country girls wanted to come to the city and be gentlewomen, and in our time they come to make their way. Both want social mobility and often use prostitution as their means.

[24]Levin, p. 23, notes that "Wires" were used as "frames for the hair or ruff"; "tires" are "headdresses"; "bents" are "frames to extend dresses at the hips"; "bums" are "padding about the waist"; "felts" are "hats"; "falls" are "collars."

[25]"Flies on flesh" symbolizes the filth upon which prostitution rests. The "gild" represents the glitter of prostitution, merely a superficial reflection. Both betray the foulness which permeates it.

[26]Levin, p. 33, notes, "Some panders were said to demand as their fee, the 'first fruits' of the women they procure for others." This seems to be corroborated in *Pericles* when Boult, the pander, procures the virgin Marina for the Bawd's brothel:

Boult.	But, mistress, if I have bargain'd for the joint.—
Bawd.	Thou mayst cut a morsel off the spit?
Boult.	I may so.
Bawd.	Who would deny it? (IV.iii. 141-144)

[27]Friscobaldo says: ". . . this old Tree had one Branch (and but one Branch growing out of it). It was young, it was faire, it was straight; I pruinde it daily, drest it carefully, kept it from the winde, help'd it to the Sunne, . . ." (II, I.ii. 89-92).

[28]Friscobaldo, in talking of his youth, says: "Wenching and I have done" (II, I.ii. 69); "I sowed my leaves in my Youth. . ." (73).

[29]See *The Dutch Courtesan* (I.i. 118-122), where Freevill agrees that prostitution is a business: "They sell their bodies; do not better persons sell their souls? Nay, since all things have been sold—honor, justice,faith, nay even God Himself—/Ay me, what base ignobleness is it/To sell the pleasure of a wanton bed?" Not unlike present-day feminists, the courtesan claims the right over her own body and declares she is in business. Whereas the merchant is permitted to sell any commodity without restraint (deadly weapons as well as necessities), society's definition of her as a prostitute constrains her, violates her personal freedom, and subjects her to punishment.

[30]Levin, p. 103, notes explanation for " 'but . . . side': She seems to mean that this is every prostitute's boast (Price)." In *Your Five Gallants,* Middleton's Second Courtesan is not a real lady. She is described as having "rustical insides and city flesh, the blood of yeomen, and the bum of gentlewomen" (V.i. 27).

[31]See Camden, pp. 122-123, who notes that while a wife is inferior to her husband and must obey and submit to all his wants, there are some situations which allow her to let her conscience serve as her guide. Camden quotes Robert Cleaver who says that the wife need not obey her husband if he demand of her "anything contrary to her honour, credit and salvation." Camden also quotes Jean Bodin who believes in total submission of the wife except when the husband commands her to do something which is "repugnant unto honestie." When Thomasine's husband Quomodo successfully cheats Easy, she believes she has a right not to submit to her husband but to assert her own higher morality.

[32]Levin, p. 125, notes that "at first" refers to "when he seduced her."

[33]*Ibid.,* p. 126, notes that "Christmas" is "implying the licentious festivities of that season (Price)." See also Alexander, p. 11, who refers to this practice: "During the Christmas holidays, almost every nobleman entertained his vassals of both sexes, a neighboring clergyman was generally chosen by him, to preside over this riotous mirth and indecent festivity, who from the nature of his office was commonly called by the name of the Abbot of Misrule."

CHAPTER III

THE PURITAN VIEW

THOMAS DEKKER

Dramatists like Dekker, who allied themselves with the Puritan position, are still convinced that the prostitute is a temptress, sinful, and to be avoided, but there is a concern for her reform. Like the Liberal playwright Middleton, they believe that wedlock is the way to make her honest. But the Puritan playwright insists that marriage be coupled with the whore's genuine repentance; only then could her problem be solved. Such repentance included humiliation and punishment. Though both the Cavalier and Puritan dramatist view the whore's problem antithetically—the Cavalier with laughter and disdain, and the Puritan with seriousness and high-minded integrity—both agree on the need for punishment. Despite the requisites imposed upon the whore to reach respectability, the male she marries is still society's shabby castoff.

In *The Honest Whore, Parts I and II,* Dekker espouses the Puritan attitude, which is historically recognized[1] but represented in very few dramas. One reason for this lack may be traced to the theatres, which catered to Cavalier, rather than Puritan, tastes. Though there are some Puritan playwrights like Heywood and Dekker, there is no other comedy, except for *The Costly Whore* (Anonymous), which treats the harlot as a central character and depicts so rigorous and sincere a repentance as that of Bellafront's. This chapter will, therefore, focus on Dekker's portrayal of the harlot in *The Honest Whore, Parts I and II.*

Critics generally find it most difficult to agree on one point of view for the work of the dramatists Shakespeare, Jonson, Marston, and Middleton, some of which I have treated here. The critical range covers a broad spectrum of opinion. But such a situation scarcely exists when dealing with Dekker.[2] My belief is that Dekker's philosophy is one that includes an acceptance of a firm morality tempered with the Christian spirit of compassion and mercy. Though Middleton may have influenced him, *The Honest Whore* mirrors none of Middleton's more casual morality, his dark cynicism, or his comic irony. Instead, it reflects Dekker's high-minded integrity, his sympathetic outlook, and his gentle humor. It is by virtue of these characteristics that the Puritan playwright Dekker is able to present such a unique, in-depth portrait of a whore.

The Honest Whore, Parts I and II[3]

My analysis of *The Honest Whore* will be directed toward Bellafront—her conversion in Part I, and the trials and temptations she must overcome in Part II in order to remain honest. In Part I, she falls in love with Hippolito mourning over the supposed death of his lady. His rejection of her trade so affects her that she is moved to repentance by her love for him. Getting the ear of the Duke, she appeals to him for justice and triumphs in her plan to marry Matheo, her original seducer. In Part II, Hippolito, who has converted Bellafront, and is now married to his lady Infelice, seeks to make Bellafront his mistress; the former courtesan now becomes the virtuous wife.

There is a Christian theme which links Parts I and II together. In Part I, Candido's patience and tranquility, his lofty ethics, and the love he engenders in others, make him the very essence of Christianity—a Christ-like figure. Candido still appears as a major figure in Part II, but a less interesting one. After his conversion in Part II, Bellafront's humility, fortitude and suffering—akin to saintliness—also serve as a paradigm of the Christian spirit. Thus, both Candido and Bellafront are exemplars of virtue and forbearance in the face of affliction, the crux of the Christian ethic.

When Bellafront is introduced in Part I, there is no doubt that she is a whore, debased, brutalized and inured to the vulgarities and violence of the trade. Though she is revolted by some of her customers, she accepts all comers:

> I, I, knock and be dambde, whosoever you be. So: give the fresh
> Salmon, lyne now: let him come a shoare, hee shall serve for my
> breakefast, thoe he goe against my stomack.   (II.i. 54-57)

Her coarseness is at once apparent when one of her clients offers
her tobacco, and she replies: "Fah, not I, makes your breath
stinke, like the pisse of a Foxe" (II.i. 83-84). Continuing her discussion with the gallants, she laments one of the hazards of her
trade, tight-fisted clients. At this point Matheo enters Bellafront's lodgings with the gentleman Hippolito, who is still mourning the "death" of his lady, having sincerely vowed that on the
weekly anniversary of her death, he will look at no woman and
will meditate on nothing but Infelice's death. His friend Matheo,
far more cynical, doubts his ability to sustain his vow. Thus,
remembering his prophecy, Matheo mentions it to Hippolito:
"Did not I lay a wager I should take you within seven daies in a
house of vanity" (II.i. 177-178). Hippolito confesses his weakness and leaves. To make amends for his insensitivity toward
his friend, Matheo asks Bellafront to help him. Piqued at the
pother created by Hippolito's grief "over a woman," Bellafront's
response harbors jealousy and cynicism: "A woman! some
whore! what sweet jewell ist?" (206). But in reconsidering her
hasty remark, she shows another side to her nature—one not
completely quenched by her dissolute existence—sensitivity: "I
warrant hees an honest fellowe, if hee take on thus for a wench"
(212-213). But such finer feelings for a harlot are short-lived.
Their existence is quickly crushed by the harsh realities of
whoredom. Matheo roughly insists that Bellafront dine with
them another night, and he provokes her by reminding her to
be dressed in the "uniform" of the common prostitute. She
snarls: "Goe, goe hang your selfe" (228).

Hippolito returns for Matheo, and Bellafront, with trade
her prime priority, starts to solicit him. Hippolito comments:
"I perceive my friend/Is old in your acquaintance" (II.i. 247-
248). And Bellafront makes her bid: "Troth syr, he comes/As
other gentlemen, to spend spare howers:/If your selfe like our
roofe (such as it is)/Your owne acquaintance may be as old as
his" (249-252). Hippolito then becomes hypothetically interested in the character of the whore, but not in Bellafront. He inquires if she would leave Matheo for him, and she replies with
a show of independence that she is bound to no man. Hippolito

continues in this vein and with a display of elitism, he claims he would not share his mistress:

> were you mine,
> You should be all mine: I could brooke no sharers,
> I should be covetous, and sweepe up all.
> I should be pleasures usurer: faith I should.   (II.i. 260-263)

Bellafront, the whore who is firmly convinced that she is a compost of evil and has long ago accepted her malediction, is suddenly thrown off her guard. Hippolito strikes a chord in her, and all the buried, hidden longings to be loved by one man break forth. She confesses she never wanted to be a common whore:

> T'has never bin my fortune yet to single
> Out that one man, whose love could fellow mine,
> As I have ever wisht it: (II.i. 265-267)

The initial step, in a very gradual and realistic conversion, is prompted by Bellafront's realization that she is in love with Hippolito. She reveals that her aspirations, similar to those of the Country Wench in *Michaelmas Term,* are to be a mistress, not a common whore. In this first stage of her redemption, Bellafront makes no commitment to morality and, as yet, has no conscious intention of turning honest:

> O my Stars!
> Had I but met with one kind gentleman,
> That would have purchacde sin alone, to himselfe,
> For his owne private use, although scarce proper: (II.i. 267-270)

Being one man's mistress had practical considerations: it would have been more agreeable, and it would provide for a somewhat higher niche on the social scale. Pragmatically, Bellafront sets specifications even for this one man who must be a "gentleman" since she is a "gentlewoman." His appearance does not concern her too much for he may be "indifferent hansome," but she is sensual enough to suggest that he be "meetly legd and thyed" (271). Bellafront is also down-to-earth about her finances, and her business arrangement would include a reasonable allowance. Having outlined her requirements with a merchant's astuteness, she promises total loyalty and sexual satisfaction. With her innermost longings laid bare, along side her prostitute's pragmatism, Bellafront tells Hippolito of her love for him: "Mine eyes no sooner met you,/But they conveid and lead you to my heart" (II.i. 301-302). But Hippolito, still involved in an academic discussion of harlotry, accuses Bellafront, and all whores, of double-dealing, and of being syphilitic carriers. But his heavy-handed accusations merely serve to bring out the best in Bellafront's nature, and she vows: "O by my soule!/Not I: therein ile prove an honest whore,/In being true to one, and to no more" (309-311). The fact that Hippolito cannot love a whore may be the catalyst in her masochistic chemistry which launches Bellafront on the road to repentance. Her conversion takes hold effortlessly; she makes no quantum leap from prostitution to penance. Her decision is simply to be a loyal and loving courtesan.

Hippolito carelessly tosses aside her new resolve at honesty and replies with a diatribe on prostitution. To reinforce her ignoble status, to make her feel that she is no more than a receptacle which one uses and thinks no more of—and which one discards by the very use one makes of it—he attacks every fear, shame and thou shalt not of the harlot. He continues to revile her and to emphasize the desperation of the whore's situation—that she merely drowns out the horror of her reality in revelry. With savage and eloquent invective, Hippolito lays bare the horrors of harlotry. He reminds her that no matter how many men the whore entices, no matter how much money she makes, there are three loathesome evils she must live with: damnation, legal punishment, and the spectre of turning bawd in her old age.

All of Bellafront's resistance is ground down. She rues the day that she first strayed: "Curst be that minute (for it was no more,/So soone a mayd is chang'd into a Whore)/Wherein I first fell . . ." (427-429). She wants only Hippolito's love and his harsh chastisement germinates into a wholehearted reverence for Hippolito's virtue, while her cankerous humiliation festers into hatred for the sin in herself. She knows he cannot love her: "I am foule:/Harlot! I, that's the spot that taynts my soule" (442-443).

Crushed by his disdain and laboring under an intensity of humiliation, Bellafront has now achieved the lowest status in the world, as she sees it, a harlot, rejected and detested by Hippolito: thus she wallows in self-hatred which leads to despair. Bellafront's desperation seems motivated by her masochism. Knowing that Hippolito has rejected her "foul" love, and that he has no amatory interest in her, Bellafront, nevertheless, persists in her fruitless attempt to have him love her. Her wish to attain the "impossible" and to court rejection, creates a self-destruction which has for its base her shame and guilt at having been a prostitute. At this low ebb, she attempts to kill herself with Hippolito's rapier, but he thwarts the suicide. Now a qualitative change occurs: her love for him has made her honest, and this revelation tears away all of the tawdriness and false reality of her past experience. She has seen a higher vision and wishes to be worthy of Hippolito's respect. Without his love, she is utterly worthless, abysmally lost; and the anguish of his contempt is such a torment that she can only beg for death. As Hippolito leaves, the spark of humiliation is fanned by his scorn so that it ignites and converts the self-destructive disdain into another attempt to win his inaccessible love:

> Not speake to me! not looke! not bid farewell!
> Hated! this must not be, some means Ile try.
> Would all Whores were as honest now, as I.   (II.i. 454-456)

Bellafront's conversion creates in her a searing hatred for all who are involved in the prostitute's trade, and in the next scene she rails against her bawd with rhetoric which parallels Hippolito's denunciation of the whore. She attacks Roger as a "Knave Pandar, kinsman to a Bawd" (III.ii. 45), and says: "I know not against which most to inveigh:/For both of you are damned so equally" (51-52). Bellafront shuns her former existence and reaffirms her vows of love for Hippolito: ". . . , beleeve me I will be/As true unto thy heart, as thy heart to thee,/ And hate all men, their gifts and company" (III.iii. 17-20).

In the next scene Matheo upbraids her for breaking their supper engagement. The other gallants regale her with that evening's events and the fine time she missed. Her response is unlike the old Bellafront: "If you be Gentlemen:/I pray depart the house. . . . I am not as I was" (34-40). Her cool reply and her rejection of the gallants meet with Fluello's anger and coarse accusations: "I am not what I was! no ile be sworne thou art not:

for thou were honest at five, and now th'art a Puncke at fifteene; thou were yesterday a simple whore, and now th'art a cunning Conny-catching Baggage to day" (III.iii. 41-44). But the taunts do not rile her. She submits to the gallant's derision in a patient manner and takes the opportunity to proselytize. She argues that whores can never have children. They contract syphilis from gallants, pass it on to others, so why waste wealth on disease.

Matheo, however, mistakes Bellafront's motives; he assumes she wishes to be alone with him, and her preaching is merely a ploy to rid herself of the others. Her seeming preference pleases him. But when Bellafront asks him to leave as well, Matheo is confused: "How's this?" (92). Her previous persuasion now becomes ominous insistence, as she restates the philosophy of her new lifestyle. The revelation which has changed her life permits an honest reply, but it also serves as a release for the pent-up anger and indignities she has suffered since her tempter first seduced her:

> Indeed I love you not: but hate you worse
> Than any man, because you were the first
> Gave money for my soule; you brake the Ice,
> Which after turned a puddle: I was led
> By your temptation to be miserable: (III.iii. 93-97)

Matheo is simply unbelieving: "Ist possible, to be impossible, an honest whore! I have heard many honest wenches turne strumpets with a wet finger [readily] ; but for a Harlot to turne honest, is one of *Hercules* labours" (100-102). But Bellafront will not be moved, and Matheo begins to believe in her conversion. She then makes a statement which indicates how ingrained was the concept that woman is basically evil, for even Dekker—compassionate Puritan—employs Bellafront to convey the well-worn fiction, as she speaks to Matheo:

> Oh, tempt no more women: Shun their weighty curse,
> Women (at best) are bad, make them not worse, (110-111)

But her following sentence ameliorates much of the sting and declares that men, too, victimize women: "You gladly seeke our sexes overthrow,/But not to rayse our states"

(112-113). Since men are also responsible, they must share the guilt, and they have an obligation toward women. Such a singular view argues for Dekker's liberal attitude and his fine sense of justice.

Though Bellafront loves Hippolito, her virtue is her first consideration. To be true to her conversion, she believes that marriage to Matheo would serve her purpose. Just as the Courtesan in *A Trick to Catch the Old One* would have preferred to marry Witgood, the man she loved, but must marry the second-best in order to be made honest, Bellafront now pursues this same course. She loves Hippolito, but she is willing to marry Matheo so that she may remain honest. At this point, her idealism is tempered with realism. Both women are sufficiently practical to make the best of a difficult situation.

Convinced that Matheo has hurt her by pushing her into prostitution, she proposes that he compensate her for his wrongdoing by marrying her. Matheo recoils at this suggestion: "How, marry with a Punck, a Cockatrice, a Harlot? mary foh, Ile be burnt thorow the nose first" (116-117). Bellafront reproaches him and stresses the male's guilt and lack of responsibility toward the women he wrongs: "You love to undo us./To put heaven from us, whilst our best houres waste:/You love to make us lewd, but never chaste" (118-120). Matheo refuses to be accountable and blames her for her sudden turnabout: "Ile heare no more of this: . . . /Th'art damn'd for altring thy Religion" (121-122). Poignantly sad, Bellafront muses as Matheo departs: "Go thou, my ruine,/The first fall my soule tooke" (123-124). She warns women to beware of men and not to trust them. Bellafront has grown wise to the ways of the male: "Men's othes do cast a mist before our eyes" (126-127). Though she is disappointed, she is not annihilated. Her new view of herself, her unrelenting desire to lead a pure existence, and her masochistic temperament motivate Bellafront once again to try to gain Hippolito's love.

Bellafront plans to disguise herself as Matheo's page and to enter Hippolito's chambers in order to obtain his love. Hippolito has charged his servant not to disturb him, under any circumstances, as he contemplates his "dead" Infelice's picture and a skull, exploiting the *memento mori* theme. Hippolito rejects a fallen, imperfect world and vows with a passion akin to religious fervor that he will be constant to his lady. Suddenly aware that his meditations have been disturbed by a woman, no less Bellafront, he reproaches her for having made him "violate the chastest and most sanctimonious vow" (IV.i. 140-141). But Bellafront is impervious to his rebukes and passionately pleads for his sympathy. Hippolito's refusal, however, suggests that his strong resistance to Bellafront covers a sensuality and a vulnerability which he protects most defensively:

> Woman I beseech thee,
> Get thee some other suite, this fits thee not,
> I would not grant it to a kneeling Queene,
> I cannot love thee, nor I must not: (153-156)

Appealing to his logic, Bellafront argues that Infelice is dead and he is, therefore, relieved of his obligation. But Hippolito enjoins her not to pursue him, and he reiterates his commitment to his lady in heaven. He wishes only to be true to his dead beloved. But Bellafront persists, begs for his love, so that she may remain upright and escape damnation:

> Be greater than a king; save not a body,
> But from eternall shipwracke keep a soule (168-169)

Bellafront continues to try to capture Hippolito's love because she still has illusions that somehow she will win him over and make him love her. The other side of Bellafront urges this campaign for self-destructive purposes. Her persistent appeal for his love in the face of his constant denial again confirms her masochism. The suffering she undergoes by this mode of behavior is the penance she inflicts upon herself for her past sin, shame and guilt.

Bellafront's last plan (though the plotting is somewhat poor) is to act mad, enlist the help of the Duke so that he may force Matheo to marry her. Matheo is helping Hippolito and "dead" Infelice, whose sleeping potion has worn off, arrange to marry secretly in Bedlam Madhouse [Bethlem Monastery]. Disguised, he is confronted by Bellafront, pretending madness, who tells his fortune; it seems a foreshadowing of their future:

> Heres a free table [palm] , but a frozen breast,
> For youle starve those that love you best   (V.ii. 349-350)

Bellafront, still role-playing, tells the Duke, acting as arbiter in the last act, that Matheo stole her "very rich jewell, calde a Maidenhead" (V.ii. 410-411). Grudgingly, Matheo admits to the Duke: "I thinke I rifled her of some such paltry jewell" (418). The Duke commands him to make amends and marry her. Matheo, thinking he has found the perfect escape, counters: "Well then, when her wits stand in their right place, ile marry her" (430-431). But Bellafront, determined to be made honest by marriage, declares that her madness is only a disguise and claims Matheo as her husband:

> Matheo thou didst first turne my soule black,
> Now make it white agen, . . .   (V.ii. 436-437)

His craft recoiling, Matheo strongly protests:

> Cony-catcht, guld, must I saile in your flie-boate
> Because I helpt to reare your maine-mast first: (440-441)

Straining no longer, Matheo seems to accept his lot, since from his dark view, most women eventually become whores anyway. The curtain comes down on Part I. Matheo, the wastrel, marries his punk Bellafront.   Infelice and Hippolito marry with the Duke's blessing.

While my analysis of *The Honest Whore* is directed toward Bellafront, a most important character in Part I, Candido, has a connection with Part II on the level of a Christian theme, as I have noted. Candido is severely tested by his first wife and the gallants, but at the end of Part I, it is his patience which "is worth a golden Mine" (V.ii. 515) and insures his triumph. Domestic dramatists such as Dekker and Heywood espoused basic Christian ethics as the true values for gentlemen, and patience is one of those sublime values. While Candido is an example of comic excess, who seemingly accepts all wrongs that are inflicted upon him, actually, he is never really taken advantage of. He is a highly moral character who sees that life abounds in irrationality, and he responds to it with sadness, calmness, and patience. Candido is not simply a humours character because of his exces-

sive patience. His forbearance gives him an inner satisfaction and
exaltation so that he achieves a mystic communion with the
divine. Candido is an exemplar of sublime values; his patience is
almost Christ-like, as represented in his closing speech in Part I.

> Patience my Lord; why tis the soule of peace:
> Of all the vertues tis neerst kin to heaven.
> It makes men looke like Gods; the best of men
> That ere wore earth about him, was a sufferer,
> A soft, meeke, patient, humble tranquill spirit,
> The first true Gentleman that ever breathd;
> The stock of *Patience* then cannot be poore,
> All it desires, it has; what Monarch more?
> . . . .
>   it is the sap of blisse,
> Rears us aloft, makes men and Angels kisse,   (V.ii. 489-507)

Bellafront's realistic conversion in Part I runs less than a
straight course. She teeter-totters between Hippolito and
Matheo, going from one to the other, until she finally settles on
Matheo, the man she can get. But marrying Matheo in order to
keep her virtuous—a man she does not love and whom she forces
to marry her—sets up a situation which will be fraught with unhappiness. Bellafront is not naive; she knows men, and she
knows Matheo. Consequently, such a marriage would seem to
support Bellafront's continuing need for self-mutilating behavior.
Her life in Part II, which is a continuous trial, evolves largely
from her need for a "hair shirt" to expiate her guilt for sins committed. While Dekker is a compassionate playwright, his Puritan
morality, in the case of Bellafront, demands that the sinner must
suffer in order to achieve purification and true redemption. In
Part II, the whore Bellafront becomes the paradigm of Puritan
values—her purity and fortitude resist all temptation.

As Part II opens, Ludovico implies that Bellafront looks
worn by suffering. Matheo has killed a man, ostensibly a scoundrel, in a fair fight, and Bellafront goes to see Hippolito to influence the Duke, his father-in-law, to pardon him. Hippolito
promises to help and during this first conversation, he admits
that he had loved Bellafront when first he met her as a whore:
"You know I loved you when your very soule/Was full of dis-
cord: art not a good wench still?" (I.i. 136-137). And she main-

tains that she has remained honest and owes her reformation to Hippolito: "Umph, when I had lost my way to heaven, you shewed it:/I was new borne that day" (138-139). When Bellafront leaves Hippolito, he reveals a new attraction for her: "The face I would not looke on! sure then 'twas rare,/When in despight of griefe, 'tis still thus faire" (161-162).

Hippolito meets Bellafront's father and attempts to soften the old man's denial of his daughter by telling him his strumpet daughter is dead. When he learns the death is a hoax, her father, Orlando, resumes his strict attitude publicly. However, when Hippolito departs, her father plans to disguise himself and to help Bellafront and Matheo.

Bellafront, now the repentant "chaste wife," is offered the chance of Hippolito's love, but she can never sin with him because he was her knight. His lament to Bellafront is: "It is my fate to be bewitched by those eyes" (IV.i. 236). But Bellafront's response reveals that she is grateful to him for transforming her, but she must shun his attentions: "You turn'd my blacke soule white, made it looke new,/And should I sinne, it ne'r should be with you" (241-242). The pattern is completely reversed—Bellafront's unshakable rejection of Hippolito and her irreversible chastity make her an unattainably desirable object for him. Hippolito thus engages Bellafront in a debate and aims to use argumentation, and by the force of strong persuasion, to turn her from chastity back to whoredom. He appeals to her emotions, prejudices and sentimental associations, and argues by analogy.

One of Hippolito's arguments is that the whore is as proud and beautiful as a peacock: "As *Junoes* proud bird spreads the fairest taile,/So does a Strumpet hoist the loftiest saile" (IV.i. 276-277). Another analogy is that she is as free as the sun. She is also rich, sought after by gentlemen, and fought over by soldiers. Hippolito's appeal is largely psychological. He is attempting to combat her feelings of worthlessness and to offset her present position of servility, poverty and abuse with romantic fallacies.

In attacking Hippolito's argument, however, Bellafront adopts realism as opposed to his romantic analogies. She dispels his arguments as unrealistic and readily evaluates the sordid state of the whore from personal experience—her remembered uneasy associations of guilt and fear with prostitution. Her rebuttal is a diatribe against whoredom, and she uses many of the puritanical arguments, so popular in the seventeenth century. Woman was created for one man, not men; men entice women with money, flatter them, befoul them, and then cast them out. The strumpet is subject to venereal disease, has no form of security, and ends up in "lust's Rendez-vous, an Hospitall" (IV.i. 328). Even when men love their mistresses, the act makes them guilty, and they get no true pleasure. The whore finds no satisfaction in her food; her bed is "like a Cabin hung in Hell" (IV.i. 356); she drinks to forget her desperation. Her closing argument—prostitution does not benefit any of its practitioners.

Bellafront's emotions, the ready result of her sordid experiences, are the real battleground of this argument. Hippolito, in the role of debator, merely attempts to weave a web of words over her unhappy recollections. In trying to substitute pomp and pride for poverty and humiliation, he makes his major error. He neglects the source of Bellafront's transformation—his rejection of her love which engendered her love for him, and her masochism which seeks out situations to make her suffer for her sin. Refusing Hippolito's love and accepting Matheo's abuse keeps Bellafront virtuous, but it is another masochistic ritual which permits her to act out her guilty shame. Hippolito, therefore, cannot win her over to harlotry—not with words, wealth, or even his love.

While Hippolito is still attempting to win over Bellafront, his wife's suspicions are aroused by Orlando, who returns to Infelice all the gifts with which Hippolito has tried to bribe Bellafront. Thus, Infelice discovers her husband's attraction for the honest whore, whom she believes is guilty. She then devises a plan to discover if Hippolito is faithful to her. She pretends that she has committed adultery with Bryan, his trusted Irish servant, and awaits Hippolito's reaction. Her husband is appalled that she has cuckolded him, and in an outcry of rage and scorn he directs scurrilous remarks at her, using this opportunity to generalize and to lay wantonness at the door of all women:

                    oh women
        You were created Angels, pure and faire;
        But since the first fell, tempting Devils you are,
        You should be mens blisse, but you prove their rods;
        Were there no Women, men might live like gods.
        . . . .
        Get from my sight, and henceforth shun my bed,
        Ile with no Strumpets breath be poysoned.   (III.i. 161-168)

Infelice cleverly distorts his tirade against women so that the
thrust is against men. Then she questions his guilt:

                    Oh Men,
        You were created Angels, pure and faire,
        But since the first fell, worse than Devils you are.
        You should our shields be, but you prove our rods.
        Were there no Men, Women might live like gods.
        Guilty my Lord?   (III.i. 186-191)

He laughingly confesses his guilt, but Infelice, guiltfree, is neither
passive nor subservient, and she lashes out at him:

        Nay, you may laugh, but henceforth shun my bed,
        With no whores leavings Ile be poysoned.   (III.i. 193-194)

Mary L. Hunt observes that Infelice's "indignant frankness . . .
shows Hippolito that unfaithfulness in the husband is the same as
unfaithfulness in the wife and that it must end in the same
way."[4] Dekker's Puritan position, clearly recognizable in the role
Infelice plays, regards marriage as a mutually binding contract.

    Infelice's jealousy, however, merely heightens the excite-
ment Hippolito feels in pursuing Bellafront. In courtship, as in
the chase, difficulties tend to inflame the hunter and add titilla-
tion to the chase. Originally, challenge and danger were present
in Hippolito's pursuit of Infelice when he married her secretly
against her father's wishes. In the courtship of Bellafront, her
rejection stirs him, and he teeters on the tightrope between win
and lose, exhilarated by the contest.

    While Hippolito is intent on persuading Bellafront to be-
come his mistress, she, in the meantime, must contend with a

husband who, in his demands for money, is also intent on pushing her toward her former evil life. Thus, caught in a vise-like grip, Bellafront struggles to maintain her hard-won virtue.

In Act II, Matheo is released from prison, and his discontent manifests itself immediately. His prison term has made him anxious to make up for his confinement and to enjoy himself: "Oh brave fresh ayre, a pox on these Grates and gingling of Keyes, and rattling of Iron. Ile beare up, Ile flye hye wench, hang? Tosse" (II.i. 12-14). Matheo's prison experience has had a profound effect on him. The sense of being confined is more firmly fixed in his memory than any of the other discomforts he suffered there. It is this sense of being caged, as opposed to the freedom of fresh air, which marks him for the man he is. Such a free character would have difficulty accepting the shackles of a marriage, particularly an unwanted one. In Part I, when in the insane asylum, he makes this revealing comment: "But heare are none but those that have lost their wits, . . . because none goes to be married til he be starke mad" (I, V.ii. 33-36). That is what makes him so mutinous and his situation so unbearable.

But Bellafront, pragmatic, and intent on reform, projects her own view and entreats Matheo to benefit from his experience and mend his ways. As yet, Matheo's feelings are still ambivalent. Basically, he wishes to fly high, but he also wants to save himself: "I will turn over a new leafe, the prison I confesse has bit me, the best man that sayles in such a Ship, may be lowsy" (II.i. 44-45). Fearful that he will take up his old ways, his wife, nevertheless, is prepared to be loyal and to support him completely, her guilt in forcing the marriage on Matheo adding to her resolution. But Matheo, humiliated that he has been forced to marry a whore he cannot endure, distrustful of Hippolito's relationship with Bellafront, and angered that he is indebted to him for his generosity, Matheo regrets that he was not hanged. Bellafront is at the root of Matheo's unhappiness, and he can never believe wholly in her repentance: "There is a whore still in thine eye" (185).

Bitter, broke, and no longer ambivalent, Matheo is desperate to live well. Having lost all at gambling, he makes demands on Bellafront for money:

> Must have money, must have some, must have a Cloake, and
> Rapier, and things: Will you goe set your limetwigs, and get me
> some birds, some money?   (III.ii. 27-30)

He takes off her dress which he intends to pawn and says: "Ile
pawne you by th' Lord, to your very eye-browes" (III.ii. 40).
She replies: "With all my heart, since heaven will have me poore,/
As good be drown'd at sea, as drown'd at shore" (41-42). When
Orlando, acting as Matheo's servant, protests: "Doe not make
away her Gowne" (43), Matheo, with a kind of restrained hyste-
ria, replies: "Oh it's Summer; it's Summer: your only fashion for
a woman now, is to be light, to be light" (44-45). He heaps further abuse, taunts and outrages on Bellafront. She knows he is a
gamester and is even resigned to the misery of losing all they
have, but she begs of him not to play her pandar:

> And when thou hast sold all, spend it, but I beseech thee
> Build not thy mind on me to coyne thee more,
> To get it wouldst thou have me play the whore?   (III.ii. 69-71)

And Matheo's rank response is aimed at Bellafront's self-esteem:
"'Twas your profession before I married you" (72).

　　Nothing Bellafront does can satisfy Matheo, and he is convinced that a whore can never be made honest. Driving her constantly to get money for him, she despairs that she will be unable to withstand his brutal onslaughts. She begs her father (un-
disguised at this point) for money, since prostitution is the only
other way in which she can supply her husband's needs. Her
father, though inwardly grieved at her pain, refuses the money
because of Matheo's effrontery and abuse toward him. But
Matheo will not relent. He heaps further punishment on Bellafront, already bruised and beaten by her trials. He insists that
she grovel to her father for money and that she supply Matheo
with meat. Finally, satisfied with the meat Bellafront puts before
him, he demands to know how she got it. Since a neighbor had
donated it, he is incensed that he is the recipient of charity and,
in a fit of temper, he attempts to beat her. Matheo's fury with
Bellafront is constantly so white-hot that when he is justly
accused of robbing Orlando, he wants to implicate Bellafront,
though she is innocent, so that they may both be hanged. Thus,
he will destroy her gratuitously. In the last act, coming before

the Duke to be judged for his crime, he tells why he wants to kill Bellafront:

> It's my humor, Sir, 'tis a foolish Bag-pipe that I make my selfe merry with: why should I eate hempe-seed . . . and have this whore laugh at me as I swing, as I totter? (V.ii. 144-147)

Matheo despises Bellafront, his wife, the whore, and his only method of easing himself is to punish her. No action is too base, ignoble or scurvy for Matheo to entertain in order to vilify and demean Bellafront, to wreak his vengeance, to ease his fury and desperation, and to employ his sadistic tendencies. Orlando aptly describes Matheo's behavior: "He Riots all abroad, wants all at home; he Dices, whores, swaggers, sweares, cheates, borrowes, pawnes" (III.ii. 158-160). But Matheo is so desperate, so debauched and so irredemable that he is incapable of responding to anything of a higher nature. He characterizes himself: "I am the most wretched fellow: sure some left-handed Priest christned me, I am so unlucky: I am never out of one puddle or another, still falling" (III.ii. 115-117). It is Matheo's hatred of his situation which is summed up in Bellafront, the object of his sadism. She is his unique misfortune, the contemptible odor that follows him like a shadow from trouble to despair, to a life of total alienation.

But Bellafront meets all of Matheo's sadistic jibes, insults and commands with masochistic patience and submission: "Oh sweet Matheo, please.—Upon my knees/I do beseech you, sir, not to arraign me/For sins which Heaven, I hope, long since hath pardoned!" (IV.i. 51-53). Her utter resignation is apparent in her comment: "Like waves, my misery drives on misery" (III.ii. 156).

Bellafront, like Jane in *A Trick to Catch the Old One,* Frank Gullman in *A Mad World, My Masters,* and Doll in *The Alchemist,* is a beautiful, intelligent and inordinately resourceful prostitute. But unlike the others, we know that Bellafront has been brought up as a lady, carefully supervised by her father. (See p. 113, note 27). Bellafront demonstrates her versatility when she acts as a page, pretends madness, triumphs in her plan to marry Matheo, and successfully debates with Hippolito on the plight of the whore. Her intellect, imagination, maturity and quick wit all attest to her cleverness, cultivation and ladylike upbringing. Consequently, Bellafront's fine background, which suggests a sound morality, brings into high relief her fall from grace to her debauched state. Such a situation would tend to inflame her masochistic proclivities and would, in turn, cry out for greater penance in the form of self-destructive rites.

In her relationship with her husband, Bellafront is ruled by force, by violence, and by masculine disdain. Her femininity is pure servility; her passivity is despair and resignation. Scorned and hated, guilt-ridden and ashamed, she has attained the depth of having nothing more to lose. Having plunged this low, Bellafront acquires the fortitude of the utterly abject. And out of this unshakable self-response of one who has truly reached rock bottom, springs an urge to live, for others—to sacrifice, to withstand trials, to embrace humility, to accept mortification—never to return to her former oppressed state of sin.[5]

Not only has Bellafront greater courage, imagination and sensibility than Matheo before whom she prostrates herself, but she has suffered while he has raged. She has the consciousness required for suffering which is inaccessible to him. And in her mortification of the spirit lies the victory of the saint. Bellafront embraces her lowliness with such fervor that she converts her odium to grandeur. The masochism consonant with her role as slave is converted to sainthood.

Hers is the moral victory of true faith, but it is not conventional happiness. Bellafront is a saint and Matheo is a sadist and their sado-masochistic tendencies feed into each other. Marriage, therefore, remains a dark struggle for Matheo and Bellafront.

The finale of Part II takes place in Bridewell, with the Duke meting out rewards and punishments. Dekker furnishes us with an excellent historical presentation of correction and punishment in this institution. The unsentimental portrayals of the whores display a realistic frankness and have almost a documentary quality.

Prostitutes, pandars, bawds and bawdyhouses were utterly repugnant to puritans; thus, they favored houses of correction which were intended to stamp out the evils of prostitution. They endorsed beatings, hard work, and humiliation which were stock practices in puritanical endeavors to fight the scourge of crime and whoredom. Though their harshness may have been extreme, most puritans were sincerely convinced of the righteousness of their measures.

Dekker's Bridewell scene is connected with Bellafront's personal Bridewell. Her master, Matheo, subjects her to the same beatings, brutality and humiliation. Thus, Dekker's Puritan morality implies that one can achieve purification and atonement for sins only by submitting to these harsh measures.

When the Duke initiates his intensified harassment of the harlots because of his son-in-law Hippolito's attachment for Bellafront, we realize how heavily the harlot is victimized. Once in Bridewell, Dekker acquaints us with the methods used for correction. The whore wears a "blue gown"; she "beats chalke"; she has "falne from a Horse-load to a Cart-load." In the name of reform, the Master of Bridewell notes that "Providence and Charity" play a part in caring for and training the inmate: "The House is like a very Schoole of Arts" where the "unemployable" or "idler" learns to adjust: "The sturdy Begger, and the lazy Lowne,/Gets here hard hands, or lac'd Correction./The Vagabond growes stay'd, and learnes to 'bey,/The Drone is beaten well, and sent away" (V.ii. 28-40). All of this is done in the name of charity and with a view toward rehabilitating the inmate:

> Nor is it seene,
> That the whip drawes blood here, to coole the Spleene
> Of any rugged Bencher: . . . .
> . . . .
> As iron, on the Anvill are they laid,
> Not to take blowes alone, but to be made
> And fashioned to some Charitable use.   (V.ii. 45-53)[6]

In a burst of self-righteousness, the Duke maintains: "Thus wholsom'st Lawes spring from the worst abuse" (54).

Infelice, evidently horrified at seeing Bridewell and the punishment meted out to the whores, exclaims: "Me thinkes this place/Should make even *Lais* [the famous courtesan of Corinth] honest" (V.ii. 254-255). The Master of Bridewell, however, informs Infelice that in spite of the castigation, not all whores repent; some become even more hardened.

The unrepentant whores bear a strong resemblance to Doll Tearsheet in *Henry IV, Part I.* Dorothea Target is a callous, argumentative harlot, scornful of gentlemen. To Carolo's spiteful remark that she "'goe to the Crosse and be whipt" (V.ii. 277), she retorts with a blend of pride and disdain: "Whipt? doe yee take me for a base Spittle whore [diseased prostitute] in troth Gentlemen, you weare the cloathes of Gentlemen, but you carry not the mindes of Gentlemen . . ." (279-281). Told that if she spins in prison she can make money, her ready reply denounces Bridewell and supports her preference for her profession: "I had rather get halfe a Crowne abroad, then ten Crownes here" (293-294). Asked by Infelice if she does not repent, she scorns the thought: "Say yee? weepe? yes forsooth, as you did when you lost your Maidenhead: doe you not heare how I weep?" (296-298). She leaves the stage singing.

The Duke examines the whores, and the Master of Bridewell explains why they wear a blue gown: "Being stript out of her wanton loose attire,/That Garment she puts on, base to the eye,/Onely to cloathe her in humility" (V.ii. 302-304). The whore is stripped of her clothes—her instrument of glory, pleasure, and self-esteem. In attacking her "vanity" and purging her with a strong dose of humility, the puritan hopes to cure the whore of her evil.

Penelope Whorehound, incarcerated for the fifth time in Bridewell, is a clever actress and begs for bail: "If you be Gentlemen, if you be men, or ever came of woman, pitty my case, stand to me, sticke to me, good sire" (V.ii. 316-318). Unsuccessful, but armed with an insolent, mutinous spirit, her legacy to the Master is: "Out you Dog, a pox on you all, women are borne to curse thee, but I shall live to see twenty such flat-caps shaking Dice for a penny-worth of Pippins" (339-341).

The whore Catyryna Bountinall's terse description of the

bawd, Mrs. Horseleach, reads like a police profile:

> Burnt at fourteene, seven times shipt, sixe times carted, nine times
> duck'd, search'd by some hundred and fifty Constables, and yet
> you are honest? . . . How many Carriers has thou bribed for
> Country Wenches? (V.ii. 374-382)

Catyryna besmirches Bots: "A Pander, a Dog that will licke up
six pence: . . . how long is't since you held the doore for me, and
cried too 'to agen, no body comes, yee Rogue you?" (402-405).
Told to be modest because the Duke is present, Kate, fearless, arrogant and beyond redemption cries: "If the Devill were here, I
care not: set forward, yee Rogues, and give attendance according
to your places, let Bawds and Whores be sad, for Ile sing and the
Devill were a dying" (431-433). The beadles beat basins as they
follow the whores about. This practice symbolizes their revelling,
while the whips used to lash them purge them of their wanton
blood. The Master explains the purpose is to calm them but even
more so, to break their spirit and exorcise their pride.[7] The belief
that the blood was the source of all humors, both psychological
and physical, may, in part, have been the reason why bloodlet-
ting was considered a cure for all diseases: the body, the mind,
and the spirit.

Bots' punishment, as the basest offender, is doubled, and
the Duke declares: "You shall bee whipt, sir, round about the
Citty,/Then banisht from the land" (452-453). As the Duke
passes sentence on the offenders, he echoes puritan morality:
"Panders and Whores/Are Citty-plagues, which being kept alive,/
Nothing that lookes like goodness ere can thrive" (455-457).

In the final judgment scene, Candido is exonerated of his
crime, Hippolito and Infelice are reconciled, and Orlando takes
Matheo and Bellafront to live in his own home.

Though Bellafront's father accepts Matheo, hoping he will
mend his ways, Orlando cannot conceal his contempt for his
daughter's martyr-like role:

> Has he not beaten thee, kickt thee, trod on thee, and doest thou
> fawne on him like his Spanniell? has hee not pawned thee to thy
> Petticoate, sold thee to thy smock, made yee leape at a crust . . .
> (V.ii. 463-466)

Orlando seems somehow to sense the sado-masochistic tendencies which act upon each other, for in his disgust, he says to both of them: "y'are a couple of wild Beares, Ile have yee both baited at one stake" (V.ii. 472-473). His forgiveness, like the "happy ending," seems a sop to comic convention, as indicated by some snappish remarks in his reconciliation speech: "what, doest thou hold him? let goe his hand: . . . away, goe, kisse out of my sight" (V.ii. 475-477).

Though Dekker attempts to deal with the whore's problem in a constructive manner worthy of his Puritan ideals, the resolution of marriage for the honest whore may be feasible but it is not a happy one. Bellafront and Matheo cannot hide the unhappiness and bitterness which exist. Even the best efforts of the playwright cannot reconcile the loosely-affixed happy ending with the sad reality.

Much as Puritan dramatists like Dekker attempted to make the marriage of the repentant whore the generous resolution of her problem, it was often too simple a solution for an issue that had enjoyed prominence for centuries. In spite of the moral fervor of Luther and Calvin, and the Protestants' proclamation that marriage was now esteemed the "higher good," a forced marriage, even to a "born-again" whore, was not a felicitous solution for the harlot and for the social discard she married.

NOTES

[1] See notes 48-51 in Introduction, p. 30.

[2] Among the qualities most praised in him are those of sympathy, tolerance, simple humanity and a romantic tendency. See M. C. Bradbrook, *The Growth and Structure of Elizabethan Comedy* (Berkeley: University of California Press, 1956), p. 123; Una Ellis-Fermor, *The Jacobean Drama*, 4th ed. rev. (London: Methuen & Company, 1961), pp. 118-119; Thomas M. Parrott and Robert H. Ball, *A Short View of Elizabethan Drama* (New

York: Charles Scribner's Sons, 1958), pp. 106, 108. For a less compli-
mentary view, which notes that Dekker knew what his audience wanted, see
L. C. Knights, *Drama and Society in the Age of Jonson* (London: Chatto &
Windus, 1951), p. 228; and Arthur Brown, "Citizen Comedy and Domestic
Drama," in *Jacobean Theatre,* Stratford-Upon-Avon Studies I (New York:
St. Martin's Press, 1960), p. 72. Many of his critics agree that Dekker tends
to moralize. See Mary Leland Hunt, *Thomas Dekker* (New York: Russell &
Russell, 1964), p. 91; M. C. Bradbrook, p. 120. Normand Berlin, "Thomas
Dekker: A Partial Reappraisal," *Studies in English Literature,* 6 (Spring,
1966), 265, contends that his writing "strongly suggests Puritan fervor."
Dekker's religious depth is echoed in the words of Mme. Jones-Davies: *"Il
choisit la sagesse Chrétienne,"* as opposed to the skepticism and worldly
wisdom so prominent in his day. See Marie-Thérèse Jones-Davies, *Un
Peintre de la Vie Londonienne: Thomas Dekker* (Paris: 1968), I, p. 86.
George E. Price, *Thomas Dekker,* Twayne English Authors Series (New
York: Twayne Publishers, 1969), p. 14, whose concepts I find most in accord with my perception of Dekker, contends that his appeal is actually
"to the individual's conscience, and he calls for the practice of justice,
charity, . . . and humility."

[3] Plot: *Part I*: This play has three distinct actions which are cleverly
entangled and finally unified. In the main plot, Count Hippolito seeks to
wed Infelice. Opposed by her father, the Duke of Milan, because of a
family feud, Hippolito succeeds in his endeavor to overcome obstacles.
Though Infelice appears to be dead in the first act, she has merely been
drugged. When she awakes, her father tells her that Hippolito is dead, and
she is ordered to Bergamo to recover from her grief.

In the sub-plot dealing with Bellafront, a harlot, she first confounds
her many lovers, and later is driven desperate herself for love of Hippolito.
It is her love for Hippolito which motivates Bellafront to give up her life of
prostitution. In order to abandon her shameful life, she resolves to marry
Matheo, her first seducer and Hippolito's friend.

In the sub-plot dealing with Candido, a linen-draper, he is a model of
patience, who vexes his wife Viola and is in turn persecuted by her. She
tries to break his patience by pretending to have a lover; she has him committed to Bedlam Monastery, an insane asylum. All the plots converge in
the triumphant concluding scene at the asylum. The Duke relents and
permits Infelice and Hippolito to marry; Bellafront is married to Matheo;
Candido is released and his wife begs his forgiveness.

Part II: In the second part of this play, unlike Part I, Bellafront, now
married to Matheo, finds that Hippolito is strongly attracted to her. Matheo
had killed a notorious villain in a fair fight, for which he has been

condemned to death. Hippolito, now married to Infelice, promises to help Matheo as well as to reconcile Bellafront with her unforgiving father. Thanks to Hippolito, Matheo is released from prison, and he promises his wife to reform and to give up gambling. However, Matheo cannot give up his vices and urges Bellafront to return to her former profession so that he may have money to continue his notorious activities. Bellafront is desperate and will do anything for him except to return to prostitution. In the meantime, Hippolito attempts to woo Bellafront but is totally unsuccessful.

Candido's former wife Viola dies, and his patience and forbearance are tested by his young skittish bride, by pranksters, a bawd, a pander, and by assorted whores and knaves at Bridewell.

At the end, Bellafront's father Friscobaldo accepts his daughter and is reconciled to his son-in-law Matheo; both come to live with him in his house.

[4]Hunt, p. 98. See Brodwin, pp. 102-103. Heywood, a dramatist with a puritanical view, takes an inimical stand to Dekker on this question. Brodwin notes that Heywood makes a significant "moral distinction" between the sexes: "When it is the man who proves unfaithful, the betrayed fiancee or wife can, without censure, accept the prodigal back. But when it is the woman who proves unfaithful, even the most forgiving husband . . . cannot accept his wife back to a shared life. She is doomed to tragedy by a societal morality . . ."

[5]See Bradbrook, pp. 124-125, who "takes exception to his [Dekker's] portrayal of women." The portraits of his virtuous women seem to have "patience" which clearly "exasperates." She finds his "good women emerge from their trials too often, like some perfect machine, guaranteed mechanically perfect under all conditions." See Ellis-Fermor, p. 125, who finds Bellafront "priggish as a convert and spineless as a respectable matron," who "is actually a piece of sentimental and cheap idealism." See Hunt, pp. 96-97, whose view differs rather sharply. She finds that Bellafront's conversion is "not the painless operation crowned with immediate material rewards so common in the drama, but a slow process involving the horror of past vileness, the anguish of rejected love, and continued hunger, blows, and abuse,—a conversion, it may be added, not at all unusual in the observation of present-day social workers . . ."

[6]See G. M. Trevelyan, *English Social History,* p. 230, who notes that as a result of the Poor Law of 1601, many "unemployables" were classified as idlers and sent to a House of Correction. See also Trevelyan's *England Under the Stuarts,* 21st ed. rev. (Barnes & Noble, 1957), p. 20, in which he

notes that these young idlers were forced to become farmers or tradesmen against their will. Women in this category would often choose to become whores, and the men would become thieves and rogues, rather than submit to the punitive regulations of this Act.

[7]It is interesting to note that whores, criminals, madmen—or all who would or could not conform to the "normal" conventions—were treated as outcasts for they were a threat to the status quo. Such "abnormal" creatures were beaten and punished so that they would conform. An example is Shakespeare's treatment of the puritan Malvolio in *Twelfth Night*. A similar treatment is in existence in the U.S.S.R. today where important nonconformists are declared insane and treated accordingly.

CONCLUSION

The Elizabethan and Jacobean drama explored the position of women, and a group of comic playwrights—Shakespeare, Jonson, Marston, Middleton, and Dekker among them—found the position of the whore sufficiently compelling to invest her with a dramatic life. Her status in society during the seventeenth century served as a vehicle for the examination of many questions concerning the sexual morality of the period. The comic dramatist projects the view of the whore into the issue of the sexual ethics of the day. Because the Renaissance theatre, particularly, reached such a large and eclectic audience, the subject of the prostitute, and the thinking which surrounded her, as projected in the comic mode, was widely disseminated.

In the Renaissance, as we have seen, prostitution reflected a vigorous individuality amid a mass of sin. And it is Elizabethan and Jacobean comedy, under its bluster and swagger, which treats prostitution seriously. It addresses the concerns of the day —the nature and position of women in general, and the whore, specifically. The dramatists often treat the prostitute as a unique, independent and significant phenomenon. Problems are posed, attitudes are probed, resolutions are sought after. In the comedies, the playwrights portray the main and crosscurrents of thought enveloping the whore—society's derelict response to her dilemmas, as well as its new-born sense of obligation to obliterate her problem and offer her a more desirable alternative. As has been noted, however, the whores are not treated with equal seriousness, sympathy and significance in all plays.

For the dramatist endorsing the Cavalier attitude, degradation remains a perpetual indignity to which he subjects the whore. She continues to be viewed as a commodity, a sex object, and a non-person. A forced marriage to a whore is deemed a most extreme punishment by the offender. Even such a disreputable character as Lucio in *Measure for Measure* begs not to be penalized in this way: "Marrying a punk, my lord, is pressing to death, whipping, and hanging" (V.i. 528-529). The harlot, while often depicted seriously and with some sympathy by the Cavalier dramatist, remains an object of derision and ridicule which is expressed in laughter.

The double standard, which militates against all women, acts in a particularly disastrous fashion to undermine the whore. Men are never held accountable for their share in the prostitute's problems, according to the Cavalier dramatist, and the female is expected to accept the greater burden of the guilt because it is assumed that she tempts men to commit immoral acts, is wanton, crafty and depraved. While chastity remains an absolute for women, men are expected to indulge not only in pre-marital sexual activity, but extra-marital as well, as expressed by Freevill in *The Dutch Courtesan*. The Renaissance male has the best of both worlds: his wife is his "lawful love" who gives him affection, while the prostitute favors his lustful passion. Not only did the whore succor the male, but he argues, as did Cato and Augustine before him, that she protected his wife, indirectly, since immoral sexual advances from other males could be safely directed to the whore.[1] One time-tested way of concealing social realities has been behind a fictional facade of semantics. The semantic deceptions are supplemented by appeals to tradition, or as in this case, by appeals to morality and social necessity.

The Cavalier attitude capitulates to all the sexist attitudes. Whores are wanton, greedy, cunning temptresses, who betray not only men, but other women as well.

Stern justice for the offending whore remains a stock method of dealing with her. The prostitute who services her male client is subject to the harsh justice which Bridewell offers. Even Prince Hal in *Henry IV, Part I,* who is accommodated by Doll Tearsheet, turns his back on her when she is carted off to Bridewell for her part in their immoral sex relations.

The Cavalier attitude accepts a wicked world and lacks a moral fastidiousness. No serious attempt is made to help the whore, for the Cavalier belief is that her function in society is a necessary one, and her way of life is acceptable to her. Indigenous to this view is the concept that the whore, regardless of personal attraction and ambition, is never offered the chance to succeed in escaping her destiny.

While the Liberal attitude also contends that the world is corrupt and evil, its cynicism accepts the imperfections with good grace and tends to work within its confines. The prostitute in Liberal comedies is wise enough to know the rake will not keep his promises; she is clever and confident, practical and assertive. The harlot learns that prostitution has too many disadvantages even for the independent woman. The punishments and harrassments, which society inflicts upon her, as well as the insecurities of prostitution, make it a difficult profession to follow. Caught in a social situation in which she is handicapped, the prostitute sometimes has the option to convert her situation, to change to a more favorable role. Therefore, the alternative of marriage, when offered, not to a prime candidate, is preferable. The reclaimed whore is confident that she will make a good wife. The Liberal dramatist views marriage as a worthwhile alternative to the whore's predicament. However, unlike the Cavalier and Puritan position, he shuns severe punishment and stern repentance.

The same injustices which face the prostitute in Cavalier comedy are still rampant in those of the Liberal mode. The whore continues to be an object of derision and disrespect; she is still considered a commodity, and humiliation is a staple. The sexist notion that women betray women is evident in *A Mad World, My Masters;* Frank Gullman's mother is her bawd. With the exception of this play, the wit still wins out and he wins the rich virgin. However, the wit begins to assume some responsibility for his whore and wants to see her make a reputation-saving marriage to some less-desirable male. Marriage to the whore is no longer faced with the same repugnance that it is in Cavalier drama. The man who marries her is generally greedy or older or a social climber and is foiled by his own craft. In the end he accepts the situation, not too grudgingly. Independent women who opt for social mobility, via prostitution, are still treated unsympathetically, as is the Country Wench in *Michaelmas Term.* However, there is a movement toward a more serious moral tone and accountability. Penitent Brothel, the adulterer in *A Mad World, My Masters,* accepts total guilt for the seduction of Mistress

Harebrain, which indicates a rather liberal view. Thus, the Liberal playwright eschews the harsh punishment of Cavalier and Puritan and opts for marriage as a way in which to help the whore to reestablish her respectability.

The depiction of the whore varies from the harsh, cynical world of Cavalier morality, to the more amoral vision of the Liberal position of an imperfect universe, on to the highly moral, though harsh, ethic of the Puritan dramatist. Dekker's drama endorses virtue and forebearance in the face of affliction. Hard work, suffering and humiliation are the only means of purification and atonement for sins. In such a setting, Dekker deems marriage the way to help the whore to extricate herself from her immoral existence, but not until she has been subjected to a masochistic ritual of punishments to rid herself of her guilt and shame. Only then is she truly reclaimed.

The degradation concomitant with a life of prostitution does not diminish in the Puritan drama, and Dekker enumerates it as Bellafront undertakes a vow to become an honest woman. The double standard, sexism, and stern justice continue to play an important part in the life of the whore in Dekker's drama. But the Puritan playwright espouses some liberal views: man, too, must accept responsibility for victimizing women; marriage is a mutual contract which is binding on both the husband and the wife. Therefore, Dekker does not condone male indulgence in extra-marital activity, as he points out in the discussion between Hippolito and his wife Infelice; she insists upon viewing adultery from the single, rather than the double, standard.

But Dekker's Puritan means to redeem the whore are fierce and unrelenting, totally in opposition to that of the Liberal playwright. For opposing reasons, Puritan and Cavalier dramatists endorse punishment for the whore. Bellafront's suffering makes a "good" woman out of her. Unfortunately, however, the conventional rewards of marriage appear to elude her, for her husband continues to believe that even a reclaimed whore can never be trusted. Marriage for the redeemed whore to society's "hand-me-down" was not the perfect solution for the Puritan playwright. Even the prostitute's pure intentions and martyr-like devotion to lawful love and husband still failed to bolster an unsatisfactory marriage. Thus, marrying off the prostitute to the flawed male served as a social tranquilizer. It nurtured the hope that the respectability, attained by the magic of marriage, would resolve the problems of prostitution. Such moral manipulation was the sedative which allowed the puritan reformer to sleep nights.

Contrary to Bellafront, Dekker depicts the common whore as rebellious, rather than reclaimed, at Bridewell, as she tries to walk a tightrope in her untenable situation. Prostitution is the only way she can earn her living, and so she is compelled to accept the stern justice meted out to her. The common quean is socially irredeemable because the well-intentioned doses of humility and the well-intentioned beatings simply turn her into a hardened criminal. Her recourse, prostitution plus punishment, remains her only alternative. Catyryna Bountinall in *The Honest Whore, Part II*, recites the litany of evils which confront her as a prostitute: bawds and pimps rule her and parasitically insist upon their share of her gains, as the law stands in wait to punish her. But her spirit is fearless and arrogant. How else could she survive?

Whether she is viewed from a Cavalier, Liberal or Puritan position, the whore, in order to resist some of society's affronts, attempts to find ways to combat the ills with which she is surrounded. Though she is powerless to overcome the force which persists in exploiting and suppressing her, she finds some ways to cope with her harsh lifestyle. The common prostitute tries to succeed in the only way open for her. However, sometimes the punishment and ignominy she must endure make her vicious, as with Franceschina in *The Dutch Courtesan*. Generally, however, she is resigned and knows that the best she can hope for is to become a bawd when she is too old to be a prostitute. Such upward mobility is not frowned upon. Ursula in *Bartholomew Fair*, and Mistress Quickly in *Henry IV, Part I*, exemplify this type who does not let bitterness overcome her.

A typical example of the whore's resourcefulness is evident when brothels are closed down and prostitution outlawed. Harlots manage to get round this edict by ostensibly opening bathhouses, which later turn out to be brothels. In this way, they managed to continue to work and to survive. Even Elbow, the simple constable in *Measure for Measure*, is familiar with this ruse.

Another form of resistance is also used. The courtesan's cleverness and ability turn to advantage the male stereotype of women. Frank Gullman, in *A Mad World, My Masters,* is quick to note that the low esteem men accord women does not exemplify women—it exists merely in the minds of the male. Gullman acts on this false assumption and turns it to her advantage. She, of all the whores under discussion, manages to marry the rich wit.

Petty acts of exploitation are another way for the whore to manipulate a situation. Since she is caught in an unequal power trap, she reacts with clever surreptitious maneuvering. Frank Gullman and Jane, in *A Trick to Catch the Old One,* are very adept at this type of behavior and use it to benefit them. They both get husbands. Doll, in *The Alchemist,* who is also clever and resourceful, seems not to lust after a husband. She appears to accept her situation without doubts or misgivings and uses her manipulative dexterity to live as fully as she can within the confines of prostitution.

Despite tries at reprisal and recourse to resourcefulness, in order to make her existence palatable, the whore nevertheless, continues to suffer under the yoke of degradation, the double standard, sexism and stern justice, imposed upon her by society. Only by subjecting her to such stringent and disreputable measures is society able both to exploit and suppress the courtesan and the common quean.

The moral reawakening in the Northern Renaissance is reflected in the dramas by giving the whore the option of marriage to the social reject, but only after all traces of her former independent existence are wiped away. For the privilege of reentering respectable society, the demand was genuflection to the establishment. Marriage was deemed a sufficient curative of her former state and a sound security against future transgressions. Such a conglomerate of punitive chastisements and castigations were leveled at the whore, that the security of marriage, even to a dubious male, was considered a prized alternative to whoredom by the harlot. But the "lumpen" prostitute, once classified and imprisoned in her role, remained an irredeemable social ill; if she tried to break out of it either by poor performance or outright flight, she continued to be alternately punished and exploited.

It is true that the Renaissance made changes in the nature and position of women which allowed her broader latitude in the regions of independence. Some of these were reflected in the prostitute's venturesomeness and improved view of herself. However, she was compelled to capitulate to the stronger force of a patriarchal society. Though women did profit from the easing of restraints on their lives in the seventeenth century, the whore could most often avail herself of the good if she relinquished her vigorous individuality and joined the ranks of the respectably married. If she opted to pursue her profession, her unorthodox status eventually condemned her.

Considering the dramatic output of this period, the category under discussion has produced some very interesting and absorbing plays. *The Honest Whore,* for instance, a two-part play, a classic of this period, is the epic treatment of the whore. It is not alone. It derives from what could be called an extensive concern or interest or absorption with the plight of the prostitute. While *The Honest Whore* represents the Puritan attitude, which favors marriage coupled with punishment to insure rigorous reform, it does not represent the more popular ways of treating the subject that we have seen in a preponderant number of examples. A Cavalier comedy like *The Alchemist* is constrained to offer a conservative view which approaches the problem "lightly," with disdainful laughter, and condones punishment, not to reform, but merely to uphold the status quo. The more compassionate concern, evidenced in *A Trick to Catch the Old One,* espouses the Liberal view and points the way to a more manageable solution to the prostitute's problem—marriage and reform without the need for punishment.

This comic mode, which concerned itself with the nature and status of the whore, also brought into focus a new and unique method for dealing with many moral questions. It permitted the playwright a broader arena in which to bare the sensitive sexual issues. This particular category made a two-fold contribution: it entertained the Renaissance theatregoer with laughter, and in revealing the daily lives of ordinary people, it served to ventilate the serious concerns connected with the varying views of the whore. Thus, the comic dramatist addressed the problems which emanated from the prostitute's existence, as well as the reality of those moral questions which her situation thrust into focus, offering them to be sorted, sifted, analyzed, and acted upon.

NOTE

[1] See note 30, p. 73.

INDEX

Activists, feminine, 111 n. 12

Adultery, condemnation of, 91

The Alchemist, 20, 21, 23, 24, 33-40, 43, 44, 63, 131, 146, 147; plot of, 66 n. 3

Alexander, William D., 18

Alice (character in *Bartholomew Fair*), 20, 39

All's Well That Ends Well, 21, 23, 24, 33, 44, 54, 55; plot of, 71 n. 22

Ambulantrices, 6

The Anatomie of Abuses, 18

Andrew Lethe. See Lethe, Andrew (character in *Michaelmas Term*), 106

Angelo (character in *Measure for Measure*), 49, 50

Antifeminism, 25

Archaeanassa (mistress of Plato), 3

Aspasia (wife of Pericles), 3

Audrey (character in *A Trick to Catch the Old One*), 78

Augustine (Saint), 142

Auletrides, 3

Bacchis (mistress of Hyperides), 3

Bacon, Francis, 17

Bardolph (character in *Henry IV, Part II*), 47

Barry (playwright), 18, 23

Bartholomew Fair, 1, 20-24, 33, 34, 38-40, 43, 44, 51, 63, 94, 145; plot and sub-plot of, 67 n. 6

Bawd, 51-53, 59, 120

The Beadle (character in *The Honest Whore, Part II*), 47

Beatrice (character in *The Dutch Courtesan*), 56, 57, 62, 64, 65

Beaumont (playwright), 21, 23

Behn, Aphra, 16

Bellafront (character in *The Honest Whore, Parts I and II*), 2, 19, 21, 24, 116-133, 136, 144, 145

Bertram (character in *All's Well That Ends Well*), 54, 55

Bianca, Lillia (character in *The Wild-Goose Chase*), 63

Birth Control, 42

Bishop of Rochester, 18

Bishop of Winchester, 18

Black Death, 14

The Blind Beggar of Alexandria, 21

Blurt Master Constable, 23

Bordellos, 51. See also Brothels; Whorehouses

Bots (character in *The Honest Whore, Part II*), 135

Boult (character in *Pericles*), 51-53

Bounteous, Sir (character in *A Mad World, My Masters*), 84-87, 92, 107